Chalk Talks

Chalk Talks

Norma Shapiro and Carol Genser

Command Performance Language Institute
1755 Hopkins Street
Berkeley, California 94707
U.S.A.
(510) 524-1191
Fax (510) 524-5150

Chalk Talks

is published by the Command Performance Language Institute, which features
visually-oriented materials for language teaching, Total Physical Response products
and other fine products related to language acquisition and teaching.

DISTRIBUTORS OF *COMMAND PERFORMANCE* PRODUCTS

Midwest European Publications
915 Foster St.
Evanston, IL 60201-3199
(847) 866-6289
(800) 380-8919
Fax (847) 866-6290
info@mep-eli.com
www.mep-eli.com

Miller Educational Materials
P.O. Box 2428
Buena Park, CA 90621
(800) MEM 4 ESL
Free Fax (888) 462-0042
MillerEdu@aol.com
www.millereducational.com

Multi-Cultural Books & Videos
28880 Southfield Rd., Suite 183
Lathrup Village, MI 48076
(248) 559-2676
(800) 567-2220
Fax (248) 559-2465
service@multiculbv.com
www.multiculbv.com

Applause Learning Resources
85 Fernwood Lane
Roslyn, NY 11576-1431
(516) 365-1259
(800) APPLAUSE
Toll Free Fax (877) 365-7484
applauselearning@aol.com
www.applauselearning.com

Continental Book Co.
80-00 Cooper Ave. #29
Glendale, NY 11385
(718) 326-0560
Fax (718) 326-4276
www.continentalbook.com

Independent Publishers International
Kyoei Bldg. 3F
7-1-11 Nishi-Shinjuku,
Shinjuku-ku, Tokyo
JAPAN
Tel +81-0120-802070
Fax +81-0120-802071
contact@indepub.com
www.indepub.com

Carlex
P.O. Box 81786
Rochester, MI 48308-1786
(800) 526-3768
Fax (248) 852-7142
www.carlexonline.com

Berty Segal, Inc.
1749 E. Eucalyptus St.
Brea, CA 92821
(714) 529-5359
Fax (714) 529-3882
BertySegal@aol.com
www.tprsource.com

Entry Publishing & Consulting
P.O. Box 20277
New York, NY 10025
(212) 662-9703
Toll Free (888) 601-9860
Fax: (212) 662-0549
lyngla@earthlink.net

Tempo Bookstore
4905 Wisconsin Ave., N.W.
Washington, DC 20016
(202) 363-6683
Fax (202) 363-6686
Tempobookstore@usa.net

International Book Centre
2391 Auburn Rd.
Shelby Township, MI 48317
(810) 879-8436
Fax (810) 254-7230
ibcbooks@ibcbooks.com
www.ibcbooks.com

Edumate
2231 Morena Blvd.
San Diego, CA 92110
(619) 275-7117
Fax (619) 275-7120
edumate@aol.com

Educational Showcase
3519 E. Ten Mile Rd.
Warren, MI 48091
(810) 758-3013
(800) 213-3671
Fax (810) 756-2016

Authors & Editors
10736 Jefferson Blvd. #104
Culver City, CA 90230
(310) 836-2014
authedit@mediaone.net

Canadian Resources for ESL
15 Ravina Crescent
Toronto, Ontario
CANADA M4J 3L9
(416) 466-7875
Fax (416) 466-4383
Thane@interlog.com
www.interlog.com/~thane

Alta Book Center
14 Adrian Court
Burlingame, CA 94010
(650) 692-1285
(800) ALTAESL
Fax (650) 692-4654
Fax (800) ALTAFAX
info@altaesl.com
www.altaesl.com

Delta Systems, Inc.
1400 Miller Parkway
McHenry, IL 60050
(815) 36- DELTA
(800) 323-8270
Fax (800) 909-9901
custsvc@delta-systems.com
www.delta-systems.com

BookLink
465 Broad Ave.
Leonia, NJ 07605
(201) 947-3471
Fax (201) 947-6321
booklink@intac.com
www.intac.com/~booklink

Calliope Books
Route 3, Box 3395
Saylorsburg, PA 18353
Tel/Fax (610) 381-2587

Teacher's Discovery
2741 Paldan Dr.
Auburn Hills, MI 48326
(800) TEACHER
(248) 340-7210
Fax (248) 340-7212
www.teachersdiscovery.com

David English House
6F Seojung Bldg.
1308-14 Seocho 4 Dong
Seocho-dong
Seoul 137-074
KOREA
Tel 02)594-7625
Fax 02)591-7626
hkhwang1@chollian.net
www.eltkorea.com

Continental Book Co.
625 E. 70th Ave., Unit 5
Denver, CO 80229
(303) 289-1761
Fax (800) 279-1764
cbc@continentalbook.com
www.continentalbook.com

Sky Oaks Productions
P.O. Box 1102
Los Gatos, CA 95031
(408) 395-7600
Fax (408) 395-8440
TPR World@aol.com
www.tpr-world.com

Multi-Cultural Books & Videos
12033 St. Thomas Cres.
Tecumseh, ONT
CANADA N8N 3V6
(519) 735-3313
Fax (519) 735-5043
service@multiculbv.com
www.multiculbv.com

Sosnowski Language Resources
58 Sears Rd.
Wayland, MA 01778
(508) 358-7891
(800) 437-7161
Fax (508) 358-6687
orders@SosnowskiBooks.com
www.sosnowskibooks.com

European Book Co.
925 Larkin St.
San Francisco, CA 94109
(415) 474-0626
Toll Free (877) 746-3666
info@europeanbook.com
www.europeanbook.com

Clarity Language Consultants Ltd
(Hong Kong and UK)
PO Box 163, Sai Kung,
HONG KONG
Tel (+852) 2791 1787,
Fax (+852) 2791 6484
www.clarity.com.hk

World of Reading, Ltd.
P.O. Box 13092
Atlanta, GA 30324-0092
(404) 233-4042
(800) 729-3703
Fax (404) 237-5511
polyglot@wor.com
www.wor.com

SpeakWare
2836 Stephen Dr.
Richmond, CA 94803
(510) 222-2455
leds@speakware.com
www.speakware.com

First published, March, 1994
Second printing, February, 1996

Third printing, January, 1999
Fourth printing, December, 2001

Copyright © by Norma Shapiro and Carol Genser, 1994
Book and cover design by Robin Weisz

All rights reserved. No part of this book may be reproduced or transmitted in any form or by any means, electronic or mechanical, including photocopying, recording or by any information storage and retrieval system, without permission in writing from one of the authors or the publisher—with the exception of the lesson pages which bear the words "Permission granted to reproduce for classroom use only."

Printed in the U.S.A. on acid-free, 85% recycled (30% post-consumer waste) paper with soy-based ink.

Reservados todos los derechos. Prohibida la reproducción o transmisión total o parcial de este libro sin la autorización por escrito de una de las autoras o de la casa editorial—con excepción de las páginas de lecciones que llevan las palabras "Permission granted to reproduce for classroom use only." Aparte de esta excepción la reproducción de cualquier forma—fotocopia, microfilm, cinta magnética, disco o cualquier otra—constituye una infracción.

Impreso en Estados Unidos de América con tinta a base de soya en papel libre de ácido y reciclado en un 85% (un 30% de deshechos inclusive).

ISBN 0-929724-15-1

Acknowledgments

*As the teacher behind **Chalk Talks**...*

The idea for creating a symbol dictionary would have remained just an idea had it not been for Carol Genser, a true artist and very good friend. Her friendship and trust have made the writing/drawing experience a real joy. Sincere thanks go to Marna Shulberg, Rick Warren, and Dan Matsubara for telling me that other teachers can use this.

I also want to express great appreciation to Jayme Adelson-Goldstein, who helped at every stage of writing with invaluable counsel and support, and to Renee Weiss, Barbara Pressman, and Susan Haskell, good friends all, who cheerfully edited the less-than-final manuscript. I am especially indebted to Sally Landsburg, who so graciously lent her expertise as both an editor and teacher and to the design skills of Robin Weisz, who also gave much more than she received. My gratitude also goes to Susan Lanzano of Oxford University Press who gave many valuable suggestions to the early manuscript and to Lucha Corpi for her help with the Spanish index. I want to express my sincere thanks to Contee Seely, who not only "liked the idea from the start" but helped see the project through with many helpful suggestions. And, I would like to say to the many teachers who have attended Chalk Talk workshops and have given me new ideas for lessons and to my students who laughed at my drawings that never got any better, your words of encouragement were extremely important.

To Mom, Neil, Eli and Alex, thanks for understanding how important this was to me.

Norma Shapiro

As the illustrator and designer of the symbols...

I won't try to fool you; it's pretty evident I had the fun part. I'm not going to apologize for it either, because my goal, then and now, has always been joy and communication, the communication of joy. Norma does that well, and she is an example of courage, humor and perseverance. I thank her for this opportunity. Otherwise, my gratitude is as simple as my drawings: I thank God for His loving Voice, my husband Gary for his willingness to overlook everything but the good, and my children, Abram and Kate, for doing nothing but being themselves.

Carol Genser

Contents

Foreword

How do we get our students, even the least talented, to be able to say what they want to say? This is a question that I have been working on for some thirty years.

When Norma Shapiro first showed me portions of her *Chalk Talks* manuscript, I thought, "This is what I do! Only it's better. It's more effective!" This is what I always thought my students should be doing. *Chalk Talks* provides the means for students to actually communicate, using words they come up with themselves while they are in the process of speaking. This is real speech, actual talking, not memorizing or parroting. What enables students to do this are the symbols (or very simple drawings). These images give students cues to the meaning and a way of practicing what they want to say. I wouldn't claim that this is the only way to achieve such communication, but it is one very effective and adaptable way. Not only can any teacher use this set of techniques, but virtually any content at any level can be taught and learned through the use of it. Chalk Talks can be used for preconceived lessons, or they can serve as a framework for lessons improvised at the spur of the moment, lessons that come from the students in multifarious ways.

Like many other language teachers, I feel it is important to use "student-centered" materials. This usually means that the content of the materials relates personally to the students in some way. In the Chalk Talks approach most of the content actually comes from the students themselves. Shapiro aptly describes such lessons as student-generated. It is similar to the very effective Language Experience Approach, which emphasizes reading much more than speaking and generally requires longer and more involved procedures.

Material relevant to your students' own lives excites and engages them in ways that nothing else can. And language that they generate themselves can't help but motivate them. The Chalk Talks approach has vital advantages that I would urge all language teachers to explore. Your exploration will carry you and your students into fertile new territory, the fruits of which you and they can't help but enjoy.

Contee Seely
Berkeley, California
January, 1994

Introduction

In ten years of language teaching as well as nine years of giving workshops and teaching language teachers, I have learned that students who are talking about their own lives and expressing their own opinions learn language much faster than those students who work solely from textbooks. Explaining the purpose of a lesson when students are talking about themselves is almost unnecessary!

How does a teacher bring students' lives into the classroom to be the topic of the day's lesson? How can a teacher turn a conversation with a student about his or her family, for example, into a lesson that the entire class can practice?

From the beginning I learned that drawing something — a stick figure or little symbol — on the chalkboard allows a conversation to develop and continue. All I had to do was start a conversation with a student about something he or she had done and draw symbols on the chalkboard. In very small steps, we practiced each sentence until each person could tell the story. Soon these chalkboard stories took up most of my class time. I began to refer to them in my lesson plan book as Chalk Talks.

The problem, of course, was that my drawings, while well-intentioned, were pretty awful at best and confusing at worst. The students liked them all right, but I was frustrated. Luckily for me, Carol Genser, a close friend and true artist, agreed to help me create a drawing system that would allow even me to draw any vocabulary word I needed for a first-year language class. *Chalk Talks* is a combination resource of that drawing system and a way to do many different kinds of student-generated lessons.

ESL, FOREIGN LANGUAGE, HEARING-IMPAIRED, SPECIAL EDUCATION— WHAT KINDS OF LANGUAGE CLASSES CAN USE CHALK TALKS?

Since I was a teacher in adult education in ESL, Chalk Talks was developed for adult students of English as a Second Language. One day in the mid-'80's, I was doing a Chalk Talks workshop as part of a staff development program in Los Angeles. About twenty minutes into the workshop, a group of junior high school teachers of hearing-impaired and aphasic students came in looking for a alternate workshop because theirs had been cancelled. Within a few minutes, they were telling me that teachers of any language acquisition class would find Chalk Talks very useful. The symbols were, they said, simple, not childish, and they were universal in appeal. The difficulty in being able to communicate and be understood was a major problem in any beginning language class, and why was I limiting the workshops to just adult ESL teachers? Since then, I have done workshops for foreign language teachers, K-12 teachers in many disciplines, and teachers in special education.

WHAT ARE STUDENT-GENERATED LESSONS?

Student-generated lessons can take many forms. Usually they are spontaneous, but some are part of a pre-designed lesson plan. Rather than being centered around a core text or a set curriculum, they are focused around the lives and concerns of the particular students in your classroom. Some are developed directly from a language need or situation that presents itself in the classroom. Other student-generated lessons focus on students' lives outside the class. Their stories, their problems and triumphs become the subject of the lesson. A lesson can also be labeled student-generated if the teacher has decided upon the topic and student responses make up the examples.

The one characteristic all student-generated lessons have in common is that they do not rely on hypothetical situations, texts, published educational materials or pre-determined visuals. They develop from real experiences your students have, and they encourage relevant conversations as well as using the ideas and concepts your students contribute.

LESSONS FROM THE CLASSROOM

What would happen, for example, if the lights in your class suddenly went out? Your students probably would talk in their native language to discuss this minor emergency. This is an immediate language need that can be used for a student-generated lesson and practiced with groups and individual students. But the conversation does not have to end here. An obvious question is, "Why did the lights go out?"

If the students offer a possibility in English, you draw a symbol on the board that in some way represents their answers. If the students cannot put the words into English, you offer a symbol and a way to answer the question. As each symbol is put on the board, it is used as a cue to practice the language. You can go back to a previous symbol and practice it. Finally, you can just point to the symbols and have the students converse with each other. For the entire lesson with teacher's notes, "Why Did the Lights Go Out?," see pages 30-31.

LESSONS FROM THE STUDENTS

When you look at your students, whether they are children, adolescents or adults, you see a classroom filled with people who have a history to tell and families to talk about. They have interesting stories to tell. If they are adults, how they met their spouses, came to this country, and got their first job are three possibilities. If they are children, how they celebrate a particular holiday, who their favorite relative is, how they met their best friend are three other possibilities.

Your students also have many problems and concerns. An adult may be having a conference with a child's teacher. Another may need to decipher information on the telephone bill or need to speak to a landlord about a leaking faucet. An adolescent may want to talk about getting on a sports team or what happens in the cafeteria. A child may have some problem that happens on the bus coming to school. It is almost impossible to run out of material for student-generated lessons.

LESSONS FROM THE TEACHER

A lesson can also be student-generated if students give the responses to a topic that you have provided. Here the focus is on one small aspect of language learning. You may be going over the activities that people do before they leave their house in the morning. Maybe your lesson is about exchanging an item of clothing in a department store. Or, you want to talk about items that can be recycled and those that can't. Because the teacher does not come in with a set list, but rather allows the students to generate the ideas, the lesson is also considered student-generated.

A lesson is student-generated these ways:

1. Something spontaneous occurs in the classroom.

2. A story, problem or concern of a particular student provides the focus.

3. Students give responses to a topic decided upon by the teacher.

ADVANTAGES IN THE CLASSROOM

With any type of student-generated lesson you maintain a very high level of motivation and cultivate an atmosphere of goodwill and friendship in the class. A student-generated lesson is not limited to one teaching style, classroom technique or learning activity. It may be a dialogue, narrative, series of questions, series of answers, sequencing activity, or even a brainstorm that becomes a chain or substitution drill. However, the situation or life skill being discussed, the vocabulary that is studied, or the verbs that are emphasized *come from the students.*

A teacher who uses symbols rather than relying exclusively on printed materials does not have to search for materials which are relevant. Every lesson is relevant because your students help you create it out of their own lives.

By talking to your students, listening to their questions and asking questions of your own, your lessons will find you. Every conversation you have with your students, regardless of how halting or rudimentary it may be, engenders symbols that go up on the chalkboard. The symbols provide the cues for the spoken language.

CONNECTIONS BETWEEN STUDENTS

Student-generated lessons also provide a way for students to connect with each other. While not all of your students are going to be friends, they need to talk about themselves if those friendships are going to develop. When they share part of their lives, they learn what they have in common, and they learn about other cultures.

A lesson about the conference with the child's teacher might bring together women who have children in the same school. A lesson on the leaking faucet might get an empathetic response from another student with a similar problem. A lesson on baseball terms might lead to a discussion about sports in other countries, and students may find out they have similar interests.

The students are encouraged to relate to each other. In a few days it is possible to ask how the conference with the child's teacher went. What did the teacher say? The class can inquire about how the relative who just arrived is doing. How was her trip? Did she have problems at the airport? When the class focuses on student-generated lessons, the students not only get to know each other, but you get to know them as well.

Every person can provide a story. Every ethnic group can have its moment. All you have to do is encourage them to talk about themselves, to tell the story of a special event or holiday in their homeland. If you use your skills as a language teacher to understand their rudimentary English, the number of culturally relevant lessons is limitless. See page 4 for lessons on cultural traditions.

The students who are participating in a student-generated lesson feel as if they are really speaking English. They are using actual events, and they are talking to each other. They have a real audience and a genuine need to communicate. The purpose of the lesson does not have to be explained.

RESPONSIBILITY FOR THE LESSON

If you teach at the adult level, using students' lives as the focus of class time gives students a peership with the teacher that they deserve. As adults, their lives are filled with responsibilities, family and family problems. By focusing on their lives, you have given them equal status and equal responsibility for the lesson. You are saying to them, "You bring situations to class, and I and the other students will give you a way to express what you need to say." If you teach children or teenagers, they too will take pride in seeing their interests and ideas providing the focus of the day.

Each lesson begins with a conversation or a discussion. For each idea, complete thought or question, the teacher draws a symbol on the chalkboard or overhead projector. The students practice the language for each symbol before the conversation continues.

DRAWING THE SYMBOLS

Student-generated lessons are conducted by the teacher in partnership with the students. The teacher may come in with an idea for a lesson, or the teacher can respond to a spontaneous language problem. Drawing symbols on the chalkboard is the key to these lessons. The symbols are the visual cues which provide the framework of the lesson. The symbols were developed for the non-artist who believes he or she simply can't draw. With only a few exceptions, the symbols can be drawn by any teacher without any practice. Also, since the meaning of each symbol is derived from the context of the lesson, one symbol has the possibility of representing many concepts. Like the universal symbols in airports and on traffic signs, the context of where they are used gives them meaning. For a complete explanation of how to draw the symbols in this book as well as how to create symbols as you need them, see "How to Draw the Symbols," page 17.

CONDUCTING A SPONTANEOUS CHALK TALK

In the beginning almost all Chalk Talks in my classroom were spontaneous. Either I began them with a planned question or some situation arose that created the lesson, and I did not know what the student responses would be. Because planning a lesson with such a high degree of spontaneity may seem difficult, I have been asked many times, "How exactly do you plan a Chalk Talk lesson? What do you say?" Chalk Talk lessons do follow a general plan. They all have an introduction, a way of eliciting the language or conversation, a method of incorporating the symbols, and a time to practice. At the end of a Chalk Talk, students usually write down the language of the lesson. And, if you look at the more specific section of "Completed Chalk Talks with Teacher's Notes," pages 25-89, you will see that all Chalk Talk lessons can have a follow-up activity to reinforce the language learned. In general, Chalk Talk lessons fall into one of four types:

1. Relating a story
2. Asking for information
3. Expressing opinions
4. Sequencing actions

To see a general lesson plan for each of the different types of Chalk Talks in a spontaneous situation, see "How to Plan a Spontaneous Lesson" on page 1. Each type of lesson is discussed, the procedure for doing that type of lesson is outlined and a sample lesson is drawn following the recommended procedure. A list of lesson ideas for that type follows. All of the general lesson plans in this chapter show what to say, when to draw the symbols and how students practice the language.

COMPLETED CHALK TALKS WITH TEACHER'S NOTES

Because some teachers may not feel comfortable drawing in the classroom, and because it may be easier to do a lesson that was already successful, I have included thirty-two lessons, one to a page, with teacher's notes on the facing pages. The lessons show the depth and variety of student-generated lessons using symbols and give you ideas for your own Chalk Talks. Most of them originated in my classroom, but some were created by teachers in Chalk Talk workshops. They are also for those teachers who would like to try using the symbols but are not yet ready to draw. The lessons are grouped according to content or topic areas. So in this section, if you are doing a unit on health in your class, for example, look in "Health and Safety," pages 74-81, in "Completed Chalk Talks with Teacher's Notes."

At the top of each teacher note page is the **source**, **type** and **grammar focus** to help you plan a lesson. Since all of these Chalk Talks were originally spontaneous lessons, the **source** tells what precipitated the lesson in my classroom. The source also shows how student-generated lessons can be derived from almost any everyday occurrence.

The **type** of lesson refers to one of the four basic types of a Chalk Talk and gives a general idea of the function of the language. *Relating a story* produces a narrative, usually in the past tense. *Asking for information* gives students a chance to practice questions almost always in the context of a basic life skill area, such as going to the doctor. *Expressing opinions* produces lists of words, or sometimes sentences, of the same grammar type or part of speech. In a lesson such as "Where Do You Speak English?" on pages 62-63 the answers give practice in nouns of place. And lastly *Sequencing actions* gives students a chance to relate the order of things, usually something that is done in the workplace or in the home.

The **grammar focus** tells what part of speech, tense or language structure is featured in the lesson. Most, but not all lessons, are solely in one tense.

The lessons are divided into three parts: the introduction or means to focus students' attention, the Chalk Talk, and the follow-up, which allows students to use their knowledge in a new situation.

To do one of these thirty-two lessons, use the following guidelines in planning your lesson.

1. Photocopy a class set of the page and give each student one copy.

2. Introduce the lesson by following the ideas listed under *To Begin* on each individual Teacher's Note page.

3. Have students practice each sentence, question, phrase or vocabulary word before going on to the next.

4. After students can tell the story, ask all of the questions or say all of the phrases or words, have them write the words on the blank lines below the pictures. (For less advanced students, have them tell you what is in each

square, while you write it on the chalkboard. Have students copy the collective story on their papers.)

5. Do the follow-up activity the same day or the next day.

If you would prefer to do a more spontaneous lesson incorporating your students' ideas, do not photocopy the lesson. Rather, introduce the topic by doing what is suggested in *To Begin* and have students generate their own answers. Then, use the "Dictionary of Symbols," pages 91-180, to help you create the symbols for your lesson.

THE DICTIONARY OF SYMBOLS

The "Dictionary of Symbols," pages 91-180, is designed as a drawing resource for teachers who want to see quickly how to make a symbol. The symbols were created over the course of many months and were tested with adult students of many different native languages. The symbols achieved an 85-percent instant recognition value. While we have attempted to make them as universal as possible, the symbols need the context of the lesson. Also, some symbols, such as those for marriage, death, and retirement are culture-based and may need additional contexts to make them understood.

The dictionary is organized by content area and many times the symbols in one content area, such as "Places to Live" or "Natural Disasters," contain an icon that is the same throughout. We have found that teachers do not need to memorize them but remember them naturally just because they make sense. As you look through the dictionary, you will notice that the drawing for each concept was reduced to the most minimal essential lines. This makes them not only easy to re-create but allows for greater readability for your students.

SHARING LESSONS

We would be very happy to hear about Chalk Talk lessons that you do with your classes. And if, in the process, you create symbols that are not covered in this book, we would be most grateful if you would send them along to us. It is only by sharing resources and ideas that our classes continue to change and be more adaptable to our students. Address any correspondence to:

Norma Shapiro and Carol Genser
c/o Command Performance Language Institute
1755 Hopkins Street
Berkeley, CA 94707

How to Plan a Spontaneous Lesson

Most Chalk Talks begin as spontaneous lessons. Students answer questions or tell their stories and symbols go up on the chalkboard. Or, a teacher can capitalize on a current situation in the classroom, such as some noise outside that is disturbing the class, and use symbols to talk about it. Each symbol represents a concept, part or all of a sentence or a perhaps one word. The students practice one sentence or a small part of the story before the conversation continues. After four to ten symbols are drawn, students practice the entire story. (For teachers who would like to use a Chalk Talk without drawing the symbols, see "Completed Chalk Talks with Teacher's Notes" which can be photocopied, pages 25-89.)

While no one can say exactly where a lesson will go, and there are literally hundreds of possible Chalk Talks, the lessons usually break down into one of these four types:

1. Relating a story
2. Asking for information
3. Expressing opinions
4. Sequencing actions

In each of them, the teacher derives the lesson from student responses and the class practices those responses. Each type, however, is conducted slightly differently and by understanding how they work, a teacher can plan part of the day's activities to be a "spontaneous" Chalk Talk.

Relating a Story

Students have an unlimited number of stories from their past as well their current lives and would love to be able to tell them in English. They also would very much like to discuss political events, natural disasters, and other events in the news. In addition, most students enjoy telling about their cultural traditions, such as what they do on the New Year or how they celebrate birthdays. All of these lessons are similar in that students are telling narratives or stories. See page 4 for lesson ideas of this type.

Your job as the teacher is to ask key questions and then transform the answers into an acceptable English narrative. The key questions are just those questions one would ask in a natural conversation. If the topic is something you have planned to talk about, introduce the topic with a story, a picture from the newspaper, or some piece of realia that you have brought to class.

PROCEDURE

A narrative lesson shapes itself. Most stories have a natural sequence. See page 4 for ideas. To allow the story to develop and have the students practice it, follow the six steps below.

STEP ONE

Introduce the topic by making a statement, asking a question or by bringing in some realia. This focuses students' attention before the first key question is asked that actually begins the narrative.

STEP TWO

Ask the whole class, or just one student, a key question. A student volunteer answers the question. Draw one to three symbols on the chalkboard to represent the first sentence of the story. You may draw symbols to represent the questions that you ask to elicit the narrative, as in step two on page 3. If you do this, have students practice the questions at the end of the lesson.

STEP THREE

Model the first sentence, pointing to the symbols as cues. Students practice saying this first sentence as a whole class and individually.

STEP FOUR

Continue asking questions, repeating steps two and three until the story is complete. As each additional sentence is added, have students review and practice all the sentences.

STEP FIVE

Students practice telling the whole story using the symbols as cues as a whole class and individually.

STEP SIX

Students copy the complete story in symbols in their notebooks. *On a separate sheet of paper,* students copy the words. This way they can still use the symbols as cues without reading the words. Students can practice telling the story in pairs and small groups.

Note that the symbols are drawn *after* the teacher listens to the response of the student and that the whole class practices each small part of the narrative before the lesson continues. It is important that all students are able to practice the story as many times as necessary. Allowing students practice in small chunks helps achieve greater mastery.

A Model Lesson - Relating a Story

If a student comes in with a bandage or a sling for her arm, for example, the events leading to how it happened become a story or narrative that the students can practice.

	Symbol	Teacher	Student(s)
STEP ONE		Ana, we missed you yesterday! Can we talk about your sling?	Ana: Yes, teacher.
STEP TWO		(To Ana) What happened to your arm?	Ana: Fall down, teacher!
STEP THREE		Ana fell down yesterday. Who can tell me what happened?	Individuals and whole class: Ana fell down yesterday.
STEP FOUR		Were you scared?	Ana: Yes, I think broken.
		Ana was scared. She thought her arm was broken. Let's practice.	Individuals and whole class: Ana was scared. She thought her arm was broken.
		Was it broken?	Ana: No, no. Doctor X-ray. No broken. Hurt.
		The doctor took an X-ray. Ana's arm wasn't broken.	Individuals and whole class: The doctor took an X-ray. Ana's arm wasn't broken.
STEP FIVE		Who can tell the whole story?	(Using the symbols as cues, Individuals and whole class tell the whole story.)
STEP SIX		Draw the symbols and write the story on a separate piece of paper. Tell the story to a partner.	(Students draw the symbols and copy the story on a separate sheet of paper. Students tell the story to a partner.)

LESSON IDEAS - RELATING A STORY

LIFE EVENTS

Why were you absent? late?

How did you come to this country?

What happened at your son's (daughter's) wedding?

How did you meet your husband (wife)?

What did you do last night (last weekend)?

What happened when you met your sister at the airport?

How did your injury occur?

What did you do on your vacation?

How did you find your house (apartment)?

How did you find your current job?

Tell us about your brothers and sisters.

What was your first job?

How did your parents meet?

CURRENT EVENTS

What happened to the president (governor, mayor, etc.) yesterday?

Can someone tell us about the flood (earthquake)?

What was the president doing yesterday?

Who came to our school this week? Why?

What happened at the Dodger game (other sports event) last night?

Can someone tell us about the bank robbery?

CULTURAL TRADITIONS

How do you celebrate the New Year (birthdays, anniversaries)?

What do you do when someone dies?

How do people meet their spouses in your country?

What are some childbirth customs in your country?

Where do people live when they get old in your country?

What happens in your country when a boy or girl reaches adulthood?

Asking for Information

Lessons about asking questions are most directly related to basic life skills. Students have a critical need to learn how to ask for information about an endless number of topics. There can never be too much practice in asking questions. This is especially true when one considers how difficult the syntax is for questions in English.

Ideas for these lessons can come from anywhere. Something in the text may spark an idea. A student may talk about a problem with a landlord or an employer. There are unlimited possible topics. In addition, it's important not to think of the students always in the "wanting" position. Students can and should practice being buyers and sellers, apartment managers and renters, employers and employees. See page 8 for lesson ideas of this type.

PROCEDURE

Students practice asking questions in these lessons. Each symbol (two or three if necessary) represents one question. Lessons tend to arrange themselves naturally from most important to least important but not always. Four to eight questions is about the right number. To have the students practice, follow the steps below.

STEP ONE

Introduce the topic by making a statement, or posing a topic, such as having a conference with a child's teacher or renting an apartment. This focuses students' attention before the first key question is asked that actually begins the lesson.

STEP TWO

After introducing the situation, ask, "What question do you want to ask this person." A student volunteer gives one possible question. Draw one or two symbols on the chalkboard to represent the one question.

STEP THREE

Model the first question, pointing to the symbols as cues. Students practice this first question, individually and as a whole class.

STEP FOUR

Continue to elicit more questions from the students, repeating steps two and three until four to eight questions have been practiced. As each additional question is added, students review and practice all the questions.

STEP FIVE

Students practice saying all the questions using the symbols as cues individually and as a whole class.

STEP SIX

Students copy all the questions in symbols in their notebooks. *On a separate sheet of paper* students copy the words. This way they can still use the symbols as cues without reading the words. Students can practice asking the questions in pairs and small groups.

Note that the symbols are drawn *after* the teacher listens to the response of the student and that the whole class practices each small part before the lesson continues. It is important that all students are able to practice as many times as necessary. Allowing students to practice in small chunks helps achieve greater mastery.

A MODEL LESSON - ASKING FOR INFORMATION

This lesson about renting an apartment allows students to practice asking questions. Your lesson might look very different from the lesson below.

	Symbol	Teacher	Student(s)
STEP ONE		Spartok is looking for an apartment to rent. Spartok, have you talked to any apartment managers yet?	Spartok: Yes, teacher. I go to three apartments.
STEP TWO		What is one question Spartok needs to ask the apartment manager?	Spartok or other student: The rent!
STEP THREE		Of course. Spartok needs to know the rent. Let's practice, "How much is the rent?"	Individuals and whole class: How much is the rent?
STEP FOUR		What else does Spartok need to know before he rents an apartment?	How much to begin?
		Yes, how much is the security deposit or first and last month rent? How much is it to move in?	How much is it to move in?
		What about a lease? Does Spartok have to say how long he will live there? Is there a lease?	Is there a lease?
		What more does Spartok need to know?	From several students: Refrigerator! Air-conditioning! Stove! Garage! Pool!
STEP FIVE		(Pointing to each symbol) Is there a refrigerator? Is there a stove? Etc. Who can say all the questions?	(Individuals and whole class practice all the questions Spartok needs to ask, using the symbols as cues.)
STEP SIX		Draw the symbols and write the questions on a separate piece of paper. Ask and answer the questions with a partner.	(Students draw the symbols and copy the questions on a separate sheet of paper. Students ask the questions with a partner.)

As a follow-up activity, have students role-play renting an apartment. Divide the class into renters and managers, and have them practice asking and answering the questions from the Chalk Talk.

LESSON IDEAS - ASKING FOR INFORMATION

WITH FRIENDS

What do you want to know when your son or daughter brings home a date?

What do you want to know if someone buys a new car (house, dress, ring, etc.)?

What do you ask someone who has a new job?

What do you ask a new friend to get to know him or her better?

What do you want to ask new neighbors after you have moved into a house or an apartment?

ON THE JOB

What do employers want to know at a job interview?

What do employees want to know at a job interview?

What questions are on a job application?

What do employees ask the first day on the job?

What questions can you ask your co-workers to get to know them better?

IN THE COMMUNITY

What do you ask when you buy a used car?

What do you need to know before renting an apartment?

What does a policeman ask you if he stops you?

What do you need to know if you are making airplane reservations?

What do you ask a repairperson before he or she fixes something for you?

What does a doctor ask when you see him or her?

What do you ask people in a car accident?

What do you ask someone after an earthquake?

What do you ask your child's teacher in a conference?

What are some questions you ask in a restaurant?

Expressing Opinions

Drawing symbols for student-generated lessons allows students to express their opinions in class and learn about each other. Some of my most successful lessons began with "What I like about ..." and "What I hate about ...." While the students learned a lot of new vocabulary, I learned how my students really feel about living in a new country.

Some lessons were more about sharing ideas or coming up with English words, and these lessons are included in this section also. These "brainstorming sessions" could be about simple things such as "What things do you put on your feet?" to more complex ideas such as "What does an employer look for in a good employee?" Basically, all the lessons in this section begin with one question which has many answers. See page 12 for lesson ideas of this type.

PROCEDURE

Any question that has many answers and is of interest to your students starts this lesson. Also, you can take the broad view that expressing opinions involves using a question which has a variety of responses. Give students some thinking time before they respond. To have the students practice, follow these six steps:

STEP ONE
Introduce the topic by making a statement, posing a problem or bringing in some realia that focuses students' attention.

STEP TWO
After introducing the topic, ask student volunteers for one answer to your question. Draw one or two symbols on the chalkboard to represent the answer.

STEP THREE
Model the first response, pointing to the symbols as cues. Students practice this response as a whole class and individually.

STEP FOUR
Continue to elicit more responses from the students, repeating steps two and three until four to eight responses have been practiced. As each additional response is added, have students review and practice all the responses.

STEP FIVE
Students practice saying all the responses using the symbols as cues, as a whole class and individually.

STEP SIX

Have students copy all the questions and all the responses in symbols in their notebooks. *On a separate sheet of paper* have students copy the words. This way they can still use the symbols as cues for speaking without reading the words. Students can practice asking the questions in pairs and in small groups.

Note that the symbols are drawn *after* the teacher listens to the response of the student and that the whole class practices each question before the lesson continues. To allow for greater mastery, have the whole class practice each response before the lesson continues. It is important that all students practice the responses as many times as necessary.

A MODEL LESSON - EXPRESSING OPINIONS

This lesson followed a discussion about how long a time it takes a person to feel "at home" in a new country. Students agreed that while some people may never feel at home, it is possible to like things about one's new city.

	Symbol	Teacher	Student(s)
STEP ONE		Many of you have been in Los Angeles over a year. Think about what you like about this city now that you have been here awhile?	
STEP TWO		What is something you like in Los Angeles?	Mahin: Food, teacher. Good fruit and vegetable.
STEP THREE		Mahin likes the food. She likes the fruits and vegetables she can buy. Let's practice. Mahin likes the fruit and vegetables in Los Angeles.	Individuals and whole class: Mahin likes the fruits and vegetables in Los Angeles.
STEP FOUR		Who else can name something good about living in Los Angeles?	Jorge: My apartment is big.
		Jorge likes the size of his apartment. Let's practice.	Individuals and whole class: Jorge likes the size of his apartment.
		Who can name other things good in Los Angeles?	From several students: Disneyland. Many restaurants. Good schools. Good mail. Freeway at night.
STEP FIVE		(Pointing to each symbol) Helena likes Disneyland. Farah likes all the restaurants. Thuy likes the schools. Etc. Who can say what Mahin likes? Who can say what Jorge likes about Los Angeles?	(Individuals and whole class give all the answers, using the symbols as cues.)
STEP SIX		Draw the symbols and write the answers on a separate piece of paper.	(Students draw the symbols and copy the answers on a separate sheet of paper. Students ask the questions with a partner.)

As a follow-up activity, have students interview each other. Each student draws what their partner says. As a whole class, students share what they have learned about their classmate.

LESSON IDEAS FOR EXPRESSING OPINIONS

EVERYDAY LIFE

What makes you laugh?

What do you like about the United States (California, Los Angeles, or other place)?

What don't you like about the United States (California, Los Angeles, or other place)?

Where do you speak English?

What are some things you are afraid of?

What problems do children have in school?

What did you like to do as a child?

What is the best place to buy clothes (a car)?

What would you buy if you won the lottery?

Where can you go to relax?

What is sad for you at Christmastime?

What is good about President (Governor, Mayor)_____?

What is the most difficult thing to adjust to in a new country?

LEARNING FROM EACH OTHER

What are things people can recycle?

Where are places of leisure that cost nothing (a lot)?

Where can you look for a job?

Where are good places to buy inexpensive clothes (food, books, etc.)?

Where are good places to hide money?

VOCABULARY BUILDING

Name items made of leather (cloth, gold, etc.).

Name items worn on the hands (feet, head, etc.).

Name items you can buy in a drugstore (nursery, bakery, etc.).

Name things you take to the beach (park, work, etc.).

What actions can you do while sitting on a chair?

What actions can you do with your hands (legs, arms, feet)?

Sequencing Actions

There is a natural order to many of the things that people do, at work, in the house and at leisure. Stories and songs usually have a specific order as well. Doing a Chalk Talk on information which students already have allows students greater ease in learning the vocabulary.

Suppose a student were late and you asked her what she does in the morning before she comes to school. She replies that she feeds her baby. Then you ask her what else she does. This is a natural place to begin a student-generated lesson. What we do before coming to school and the order in which we do these things is a good lesson for sequencing. The students should number the steps after the lesson if they do the same things in a different order. See page 16 for lesson ideas of this type.

PROCEDURE

Any sequence that has more than four or five steps and is of interest to your students can work. You can use sequencing to tell what happened in a story or song. Use it also for the steps to follow when making or building something. See page 16 for lesson ideas.

Part of the procedure is to have students put the sequence into the correct order. Your students may have lively discussions on the correct order of the sequence.

STEP ONE

Introduce the topic by making a statement, asking a question or bringing in some realia. This focuses students' attention before the "first question" is asked that actually begins the lesson.

STEP TWO

Ask one student volunteer to give a possible step in the sequence. (You may attempt to do the sequence in order or just take the steps randomly.) Draw one or two symbols on the chalkboard to represent that step.

STEP THREE

Model the first item in the sequence, pointing to the symbols as cues. Students practice the first item, individually and as a whole class.

STEP FOUR

Continue to elicit additional parts of the sequence, repeating steps two and three until you have completed the sequence. As each additional response is added, have students review and practice all the responses.

STEP FIVE

Have a student volunteer number the steps. Discuss the correct order. Discuss different opinions about the order. Have students practice all the steps in the sequence using the symbols as cues.

STEP SIX

Students copy the sequence in symbols in the correct order in their notebooks. *On a separate sheet of paper* students copy the words. This way they can still use the symbols as cues without reading the Students can practice saying the sequence in pairs and in small groups.

Note that the symbols are drawn *after* the teacher listens to the response of the student and that the whole class practices each step in the sequence before the lesson continues. To allow for greater mastery, have the whole class practice each response before the lesson continues. It is important that all students practice the sequence as many times as necessary. Allowing students to practice in small chunks helps achieve greater mastery.

A MODEL LESSON - SEQUENCING ACTIONS

This lesson about the morning routine of one student allows students to practice common verbs. The steps are not yet in order. Rather than rewriting all the symbols, they are numbered at the end of the lesson.

	Symbol	Teacher	Student(s)
STEP ONE		Everyone does different things in the morning. Alta, think about what you do every morning.	Alta: I do a lot of things teacher!
STEP TWO		What is something you do every morning?	Alta: I feed my baby.
STEP THREE		Alta feeds her baby every morning. Let's practice. Alta feeds her baby every morning.	Individuals and whole class: Alta feeds her baby every morning.
STEP FOUR		What else do you do every morning? Can you name something else?	Alta: I have a cup of coffee.
		Alta has a cup of coffee every morning. Let's practice.	Individuals and whole class: Alta has a cup of coffee.
		What else do you do every morning before you come to school?	Alta: I get dressed. Oh, I wake up! Sometimes I do the dishes from the night before. I like a hot shower.
STEP FIVE		(Pointing to each symbol) Alta gets dressed. She wakes up. Sometimes she does the dishes from the night before. She likes a hot shower. Let's put numbers in the correct order next to what Alta does.	(Individuals offer possibilities of the correct order. The whold class practice saying the whole sequence, using the symbols as cues.)
STEP SIX		Draw the symbols in the order you believe is the most correct. Copy what Alta does on a separate sheet of paper.	(Students draw the symbols and copy the sequence on a separate sheet of paper. Students practice the sequence with a partner.)

As a follow-up have each student draw all the things they do before they come to school. Have them share with a partner their morning routine.

LESSON IDEAS - SEQUENCING ACTIONS

EVERYDAY LIFE

How to paint a house (plant a garden, etc.).

How to make a dress (bookcase, etc.).

How to make an omelet (rice, etc.).

How to use a pay telephone (microwave, etc.).

How to fix a tire (lamp, etc.).

What you do when you write and mail a letter?

What do you do when you take a pill?

What do you do when you wash your hands (dishes, clothes)?

What do you need to do before (after) you give a party?

What do you do before you leave the house?

How do you clean your house?

What do you do when you go to a party?

What do you do before (after) you exercise?

AT WORK

How to use a copy machine (fax machine, etc.).

What does a bank robber do before he robs a bank?

What does a jockey do before he rides his horse?

What does a soccer player do before a big game?

AT SCHOOL

What you do when you come to school?

What happened to _____ in the story?

What happened to _____ in the song?

How do you get ready to study English?

How to Draw the Symbols

The symbols were developed for people who believe that drawing, even drawing a simple stick figure, is difficult. Each symbol is pared down to the minimum number of lines, many have a similar foundations.

Drawing the symbols should be as easy as writing the alphabet. If you practice them a few times, you will be able to produce them quickly anytime you need them. For some action symbols such as walking and running, stick figures are used.

Use the following guidelines to draw the symbols most easily and have them understood.

1. Use one symbol to represent a concept, a sentence or an idea, *not* a word.

"How much does the car cost?" in symbols might be this:

If everyone understands that the entire lesson is about buying an automobile, this would suffice:

In other words, use as few symbols as you can get away with. The symbols are there only to represent cues for language that is *already understood*, not for teaching vocabulary concepts.

2. Use the fewest lines possible.

Don't spend time drawing ears, fingers, hats, hair, or even legs for that matter, if these items aren't necessary for understanding. If you are drawing a character for a dialogue and want to be creative, go ahead, but symbols for Chalk Talks are best when they are drawn simply and fast.

man

good

too detailed

hand

good

confusing

eat

good

confusing

3. Use similar symbols for related concepts.

Symbols on the same subject have a common icon throughout. This makes them easier to remember and easier for the students to recognize them.

common icons

places/building

time

disasters

pain

emergencies

occupations

4. Make mistakes.

This shows that you have a sense of humor and are not embarrassed to try something new. Five lumps is a hand. It does not matter if it has an opposing thumb or not. Four lumps can be a hand if you miscount.

hand

5. Add emotions to the people to help convey meaning.

Many times the emotional response will be the key to understanding for your students. For more symbols of emotions, see pages 100-101.

Spartok has
an earache.

Helena lost
her job.

Mario has
a girlfriend.

Paulo got a letter
from his father.

6. Use one symbol to stand for many words or concepts.

It might seem confusing for one symbol to have so many possible meanings but it is not. The context of the lesson give the symbols their meaning and allow them to be cues for practicing speaking.

money, pay, cost, rich, paycheck, cash, buy, sell

hear, listen, pay attention, noise, noisy, sound

7. Use nouns to represent verbs.

to iron

difficult to draw

easy to draw

to cut

difficult to draw

easy to draw

8. Exaggerate for effect.

This is similar to drawing the emotional response. It allows for a great variety of meaning without having to know more symbols.

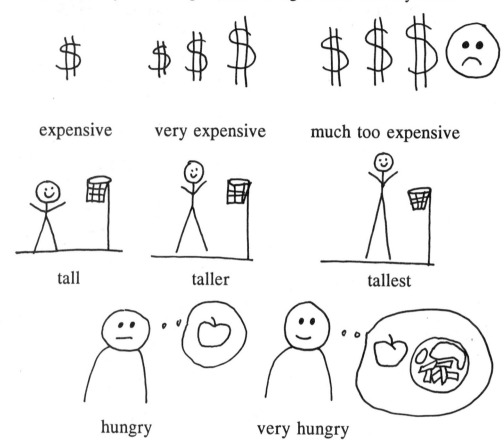

expensive   very expensive   much too expensive

tall   taller   tallest

hungry   very hungry

9. Draw from the top down.

It is usually easier, and many times you can stop drawing after you have drawn just the head and shoulders.

10. Draw the foreground first and then draw the background.

It prevents some erasing. Also, when you draw things behind other things, you can leave out some lines.

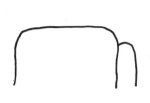  

11. Learn a few cartooning specialties.

speed   movement   exaggeration

What happens if you are stuck?

What happens if you are in the middle of a lesson and you just plain get stuck? Suddenly you just can't think of a way to draw a symbol you need, and it's not in the lessons or the dictionary. Some words difficult to symbolize are "idea words" such as justice, poverty, healthcare. Other words difficult to put into symbols are words such as immigration office, insurance, crime. What do you do?

If you are stuck, you can always write the word in English. Or, you can write down a possible symbol, such as a big building for court and write the word near it. You can also just write down a squiggly line and just tell students that this stands for crime. And lastly, you can ask the students (who by now are used to your drawings) to draw the word for you.

Students are going to appreciate your efforts no matter what your symbols look like. You are drawing, after all, pictures about their lives so that they can learn English. They will see your drawings, however unartistic, as gifts to help them learn.

GUIDELINE REVIEW FOR DRAWING THE SYMBOLS

1. Use one symbol to represent a concept, a sentence or an idea, not a word.

2. Use the fewest lines possible.

3. Use similar symbols for related concepts.

4. Make mistakes.

5. Add emotions to the people to help convey meaning.

6. Use one symbol to stand for many words or concepts.

7. Use nouns to represent verbs.

8. Exaggerate for effect.

9. Draw from the top down.

10. Draw the foreground first and then draw the background.

11. Learn a few cartooning specialties, such as speed lines, movement lines and exaggeration.

Completed Chalk Talks
with Teacher's Notes

The First Day of Class

I use the symbols even on the first day of class with beginning and intermediate students. With these symbols students practice asking those "first day" questions they may have. I also like to teach some clarification strategy, such as, "I don't understand." We also practice saying the answers.

SOURCE	I thought of this lesson as a way to give students essential information.
TYPE	Asking for information
GRAMMAR FOCUS	Present tense, questions

TO BEGIN Draw Symbol 1 on the board. Ask students their names. Give your name. Extend your hand for a handshake. Do this for every student.

CHALK TALK

1. **What's your name?**

2. **What level is this?**

3. **How long is the class?**

4. **Where do I sit?**

5. **Where is the bathroom?**

6. **When is the break?**

7. **How much is the book?**

8. **I don't understand.**

TO FOLLOW UP Practice these questions every day the first week of class and as new students register. (You may want to put these symbols as well as new ones that come up during the discussion on a large posterboard or tearsheet for the first week of school.) Also, give students additional ways to ask for clarification, to ask the speaker to speak more slowly, etc.

The First Day of Class

1.	2.
3.	4.
5.	6.
7.	8.

_____

_____

_____

_____

_____

_____

_____

  Permission granted to reproduce for classroom use only.

Late to Class

This lesson can take place the second or third week of class of an advanced beginning or low intermediate class. A student who is usually in class is missing. The teacher and class are not sure if the student is late or absent. The class learns how to give reasons for being absent.

SOURCE   A student who was usually on time was not in his seat at the start of class.

TYPE   Expressing opinions

GRAMMAR FOCUS   Expressing possibility, simple present, simple past

TO BEGIN   The teacher focuses this lesson by pointing to the empty chair and asking, "Where is _____ today? Does anyone know?"

CHALK TALK   1. Where is _____ ?

2. Maybe he missed the bus.

3. Maybe he slept late.

4. Maybe his car didn't start.

5. Maybe he went to work and is not coming today.

6. Maybe he is sick.

7. Maybe someone in the family is sick.

8. It's a secret.

TO FOLLOW UP   Discuss acceptable and not acceptable reasons for missing school in students' homelands and in the United States. Write two headings with these two categories on the chalkboard: Acceptable reasons and Not acceptable. Have students come to the board and draw the symbols from the lesson under the category they feel is appropriate.

1.

2.

3.

4.

5.

6.

7.

8.

_____

_____

_____

_____

_____

_____

_____

_____

Permission granted to reproduce for classroom use only.

Why Did the Lights Go Out?

When the lights in my class suddenly went out, all of my students began to speak at once in their native languages. Such an immediate language need made for an immediate student-generated lesson. Lessons that are derived from spontaneous classroom occurrences almost need no introduction.

SOURCE	The lights in class suddenly went out.
TYPE	Expressing opinions
GRAMMAR FOCUS	Expressing possibility, simple present, simple past, past perfect
TO BEGIN	Draw the first symbol on the chalkboard. Ask students, "What happened?"
CHALK TALK	**1. The lights went out.** **2. Why did the lights go out? Does anybody know?** **3. Maybe the school didn't pay the electricity bill?** **4. Maybe the power line has fallen.** **5. Maybe someone is fixing the line and the power is off.** **6. Maybe we need a new lightbulb.**
TO FOLLOW UP	Have students, in pairs or small groups, brainstorm a list of other problems that might happen in class. Students can draw symbols or can write the words in their new language. Possible answers: 1. leaking roof 2. fire 3. broken window 4. cockroaches 5. broken lock 6. mouse

Why Did the Lights Go Out?

1.

2.

3.

4.

5.

6.

_____

_____

_____

_____

_____

_____

_____

     Permission granted to reproduce for classroom use only.

Problems in School

I had conducted a survey asking students where they wanted to use English the most. I learned that my ESL adult students who had children in public school wanted to be able to speak better English at teacher/parent conferences. Also, this lesson is very relevant for the teacher who needs to explain to students from elementary through high school how to do better in school.

SOURCE An adult student was having a parent-teacher conference and wanted to be able to talk with her child's elementary school teacher.

TYPE Expressing opinions

GRAMMAR FOCUS Expressing possibility, simple present

TO BEGIN Focus students' attention by bringing in a report card from an elementary, middle or high school. Write the subjects and grades on the chalkboard. Ask students, "Why is the student having a hard time at school? What do you think the problem is?"

CHALK TALK
1. **Maybe she doesn't pay attention.**

2. **Maybe she talks too much to her friends.**

3. **Maybe she doesn't understand the assignments.**

4. **Maybe she doesn't do her homework.**

5. **Maybe she is lonely and doesn't have friends.**

6. **Maybe she needs glasses.**

TO FOLLOW UP Divide students into six groups. Give each group a large sheet of butcher paper. Assign each group one of the above problems and have them brainstorm solutions to that problem. Depending on the level, have them draw symbols or write words to represent their answers. After ten to twenty minutes have each group post their butcher paper with their solutions around the room and share their answers.

Permission granted to reproduce for classroom use only.

How Guadalupe Met Her Husband

Guadalupe was the oldest student in my class, probably close to eighty. We were talking about the verb "to meet." I don't know what prompted me to ask Guadalupe this question, but I did. "Guadalupe," I said, "do you remember how you met your husband?" Guadalupe, a widow for over twenty years, turned fifteen before our eyes.

SOURCE	A student recalled an important moment in her life.
TYPE	Relating a story
GRAMMAR FOCUS	Simple past tense

TO BEGIN — Tell the class that the day's lesson is about random pleasant memories. Ask if they remember a time when something special happened. You may need to prompt students with more specific questions, such as the one I asked Guadalupe to begin the story.

CHALK TALK

1. Guadalupe lived in a small town near San Salvador.

2. Jorge lived a few miles away.

3. One day Jorge and his father came to deliver milk in a donkey cart.

4. Guadalupe saw him.

5. She thought he was handsome.

6. Every morning when he came, she hid behind the door of her house.

7. After four days, she finally came out and said hello.

TO FOLLOW UP — Discuss cultural differences about acceptable ways young people can meet people in this country and in the students' homelands.

How Guadalupe Met Her Husband

 Permission granted to reproduce for classroom use only.

Why Paulo Came to the United States

While this lesson may look short and perhaps simple, it is representative of many student-generated lessons on the same topic, how and why students come to the United States. Not all students may want to share their story with the class. Some of course, are much more painful and difficult than Paulo's. Still, each student can draw his or her own personal story and share the story with a classmate.

SOURCE A student recalled why he came to the United States.

TYPE Relating a story

GRAMMAR FOCUS Simple past tense

TO BEGIN Ask the class if anyone would like to tell why he or she came to the United States.

CHALK TALK

1. **Paulo went to a school in Rio de Janeiro.**

2. **He liked learning English.**

3. **Everyone said he should go to the United States to learn more English.**

4. **Paulo saved money for four years for the plane ticket.**

5. **At last he wrote to his uncle in the United States.**

6. **His uncle gave him a job in his restaurant in the United States.**

7. **In the morning Paulo works at the restaurant.**

8. **At night he goes to school.**

TO FOLLOW UP Have a student volunteer to be "Paulo." Brainstorm questions the class can ask Paulo now that everyone knows his story, such as, "Are you still working for your uncle?" Practice more questions with *still*. "Do you still save money?" "Do you still like learning English?"

Why Paulo Came to the United States

 Permission granted to reproduce for classroom use only.

Why Sara Came to the United States

I am always prepared to do a lesson about how students come to the United States. This may happen any time during the semester as we have open enrollment and we are always accepting new students into our school. Sara came to class while we were talking about family. It was during a discussion about who lives at home that Sara told her story.

SOURCE A student told the class that she is the only person from her immediate family who had come to live in the United States.

TYPE Relating a story

GRAMMAR FOCUS Past tense

TO BEGIN Draw one student with an outline of her native country and her homeland. Draw the appropriate family members in each outline.

CHALK TALK
1. **Sara's life in Guatemala was not easy.**

2. **She has many brothers and sisters, and there was not much work.**

3. **She wrote to her cousin in the United States.**

4. **He sent her money to buy a plane ticket.**

5. **Sara now works cleaning houses. She sends money to her parents in Guatemala.**

6. **She really misses her family.**

TO FOLLOW-UP Divide the class into groups of four to conduct an interview. Decide on three or four questions, such as, "Where are you from?", "How long have you been in the United States?", "Who do you live with?" and "Where does your family live?" Have students take turns asking each person in the group a different question while the other students write the answers.

*This activity was adapted from The New Oxford Picture Dictionary Listening and Speaking Activity Book by Jayme Adelson-Goldstein, Rita Goldman, Norma Shapiro and Renee Weiss.

Why Sara Came to the United States

How Ismael Crossed the Mountains

When my student Ismael told this story to the class, it was the catalyst that allowed other students to tell of their difficult passages to the United States. With Ismael's permission, I asked many questions that allowed the story to progress such as, "How did you feel?", "What did you take?" and "How long did you travel through the mountains?"

SOURCE A student told the class that coming to the United States was the most difficult thing he had ever done.

TYPE Relating a story

GRAMMAR FOCUS Past tense

TO BEGIN Focus students' attention by showing students where Afghanistan is on a world map. Point out the mountains inside the country and the route to Pakistan. Talk about the size of the mountains and the distance between the two countries.

CHALK TALK

1. Ismael lived in Afghanistan.

2. In 1979 many soldiers from the Soviet Union went into Afghanistan.

3. In 1983 Ismael had to join the army.

4. He was afraid and very nervous.

5. He couldn't sleep or eat.

6. He packed some papers, some jewelry and food.

7. He walked through the mountains. It took four days.

8. Finally he made it to Pakistan.

TO FOLLOW-UP With the students, brainstorm a list of reasons why people become emigrants. Try to include some reasons that represent individual choice as well as those of survival.

How Ismael Crossed the Mountains

Permission granted to reproduce for classroom use only.   41

What José Does Before School

There are many lessons about daily routines. After doing one such lesson in our text, we had a discussion about who takes care of the children in the morning. José said he loves to help the children in the morning because he thinks they are the nicest then.

SOURCE	The class had completed a sequence about morning routines. Students agreed that everyone's morning routine was a little different.
TYPE	Sequencing
GRAMMAR FOCUS	Present tense, third person singular
TO BEGIN	Ask the class general questions about their morning routine, such as, "How many drink coffee in the morning?" or "How many do housework in the morning?"
CHALK TALK	1. José wakes up at 6:00.
	2. He makes coffee and smokes a cigarette.
	3. Then he drinks his coffee.
	4. Then he wakes up his children.
	5. He gives the children breakfast...
	6. ...and gets dressed.
	7. He kisses his wife goodbye...
	8. ...and takes the children to school.
TO FOLLOW-UP	Have the students draw the sequence of their own morning routine, what they do after school or how they spend Saturday or Sunday. Have them share their story with a partner or a small group.

What José Does Before School

Louisa's Vacation

This lesson was the first of many such Monday morning discussions that began, "What did you do this weekend?" The sentences for these lessons are sometimes a little longer, and so I run the symbols across the chalkboard for each sentence.

SOURCE — Louisa had come to class one Monday morning after being absent.

TYPE — Relating a story

GRAMMAR FOCUS — Past tense

TO BEGIN — Express concern to a student who was absent from class. Ask if they would like to tell the class why they were absent. Another possibility is to ask students what they did over the weekend.

CHALK TALK

1. **Last week Louisa went to Palm Springs for four days.**

2. **Louisa didn't like it because it was too hot.**

3. **The children went swimming, but Louisa didn't go because she can't swim.**

TO FOLLOW UP — Brainstorm lists of sports. As students name the sports, draw a symbol for each one. Have students copy the symbols on a piece of paper and add sports symbols of their own. Have students work with partners or in small groups and ask "can you" questions.

Louisa's Vacation

1.

2.

3.

_____

_____

_____

_____

_____

_____

_____

Permission granted to reproduce for classroom use only.

Buying a Used Car

During a Monday morning warm-up, Thang, a student from Vietnam, told us how he went looking for a used car. We started talking about how to buy a used car and that became the first lesson of the day. By the week's end we had done a lesson about abbreviations in car ads, one on car repair and had done a role-play on both buying a used car and taking it for repairs.

SOURCE	A student told the class about going to buy a used car.
TYPE	Asking for information
GRAMMAR FOCUS	Interrogative form

TO BEGIN Focus students' attention by bringing in newspaper ads from the classified section on used cars. Tell students the class will be practicing asking questions of the used car salesman.

CHALK TALK

1. **What is the asking price of the car?**

2. **How many miles does it have?**

3. **How much are the monthly payments?**

4. **Is there a warranty?**

5. **Was the car ever in an accident?**

6. **How old are the tires?**

TO FOLLOW UP Role-play the process of buying a used car. Divide the class into buyers and sellers. Have students who are sellers draw a car they would like to sell and decide on a price. Have students who are buyers walk around and ask about the cars as if they were going to purchase them.

This activity was adapted from The New Oxford Picture Dictionary Listening and Speaking Activity Book by Jayme Adelson-Goldstein, et al.

Permission granted to reproduce for classroom use only.

Sook's Reunion With Her Sister

There are many lessons about family. Admittedly, there wasn't a dry eye when Sook came to class and told us about the reunion with her sister the previous Wednesday. Afterward, we asked Sook many questions about her sister. "Did she seem the same?" "How long is she staying?" "What does she like about the United States?" "What doesn't she like about the United States?" It was a lot of fun to hear Sook tell her story.

SOURCE
A student told us about how she went to the airport to pick up her sister.

TYPE
Relating a story

GRAMMAR FOCUS
Past tense

TO BEGIN
Focus students' attention by showing them where Korea is on a world map. Draw the outline of Korea and the United States on the chalkboard. Show those family members who live in the United States and those who live in Korea.

CHALK TALK
1. Sook came to the United States many years ago.

2. She last saw her sister in 1951.

3. Last month Sook got a letter from her sister.

4. Her sister wrote that she is coming to the United States.

5. Last Wednesday, Sook and her family went to the airport.

6. They were very excited.

7. When they met Sook's sister, everyone cried and hugged each other.

TO FOLLOW UP
Have students draw a picture of someone in their family that they would like to see. Have them tell a partner about this person.

Sook's Reunion With Her Sister

A Plane Crash in Iowa

We were doing a unit on safety procedures in disasters when this item was in the news. Before we talked about what to do in a plane crash, I did this lesson as an introduction. Luckily some of my students had heard about this on the radio. Even if they hadn't, I would have told the story to them, drawing the symbols as I went along.

SOURCE The newspaper carried the story of a plane crash in Iowa.

TYPE Relating a story

GRAMMAR FOCUS Past tense

TO BEGIN Ask the class if anyone heard about the plane crash. Show them a picture of a map and draw the symbol for the plane crash.

CHALK TALK
1. There was a terrible storm yesterday.

2. A plane crashed in Iowa.

3. 83 people were injured.

4. Luckily, there was no fire.

5. Luckily, the plane landed in a corn field.

6. Many family and friends were nervous as they waited in the airport.

TO FOLLOW UP Talk about safety procedures in a plane, such as where to store your lugguage, how to count the number of rows to the nearest exit in case of smoke, and keeping alcohol use to a minimum.

A Plane Crash in Iowa

Earthquake in Mexico City

When my students came to class after the earthquake in Mexico City in October of 1987, I knew that we needed to talk about it. Students who were not from Mexico and I needed to express our concern. We needed to ask the Mexican students how their families were and to say how sorry we were. When my students came in that day and for several days afterward, there was talk of little else.

If, unfortunately, a disaster strikes where some of your students have family, you can talk about this in your class. While this may seem like simple pictures for expressing concern and sorrow, students appreciate being able to say in English what they are thinking in their native language. If you are doing this lesson not based on an actual news event, you might have to ask your class to imagine what questions would be asked if an earthquake or other natural disaster occurred where friends have family.

SOURCE	An earthquake hit Mexico City. Many students had family living there.
TYPE	Asking for information, expressing concern
GRAMMAR FOCUS	Present tense, questions
TO BEGIN	Draw Symbol 1 on the board. Pantomime an earthquake happening.
CHALK TALK	**1. There was an earthquake in Mexico City yesterday. We are so sorry.**
	2. Did you hear from your family?
	3. How are they?
	4. What do they need?
	5. Tell us as soon as you hear something.
TO FOLLOW UP	The next day, conduct a lesson on the rescue efforts. Talk about what people do after an earthquake to help the victims.

Earthquake in Mexico City

Earthquake in Los Angeles

When we had an earthquake in Los Angeles in January of 1994, we did this lesson the next day. As often is the case with big news events, I brought in the front section of the newspaper.

SOURCE	An earthquake hit in our city, Los Angeles.
TYPE	Asking for information (expressing concern)
GRAMMAR FOCUS	Present and past tense, questions

TO BEGIN   Bring in a newspaper about the event. Draw Symbol 1 on the chalkboard.

CHALK TALK

1. **Where were you when the earthquake happened?**

2. **Is your family okay?**

3. **Did anything break in your home?**

4. **Is your telephone working?**

5. **Do you have electricity?**

6. **Were you scared?**

TO FOLLOW UP   Brainstorm safety procedures on what to do before an earthquake or other disaster. Other lessons might include what to do during and after an earthquake and what supplies to have in an earthquake kit.

Earthquake in Los Angeles

1.

2.

3.

4.

5.

6.

Permission granted to reproduce for classroom use only.

A Bank Robbery at State National Bank

The newspaper can probably provide material for lessons every day of the year. There was a robbery close to the school. My intent was not just to teach the story of the robbery, but to go on to teach a lesson about crime prevention.

SOURCE	There was an account of a bank robbery in the newpaper.
TYPE	Relating a story
GRAMMAR FOCUS	Simple past tense

TO BEGIN	Bring in a newspaper about the event. Draw Symbol 1 on the chalkboard.
CHALK TALK	**1. There was a robbery at State National Bank.**
	2. The robbers gave a note to the teller.
	3. Everyone was scared.
	4. They lay down on the floor.
	5. The teller put the money in a suitcase and pressed the button.
	6. When the police came, the robbers were gone.
TO FOLLOW UP	Conduct a discussion on different types of crime and how to avoid being a victim. Cover such topics as where to keep money safely and how to safeguard your valuables. If possible, invite a police officer to talk to the class.

A Bank Robbery at State National Bank

What Do You Do on a Hot Day?

This is the simplest of all lessons. Here is one question with the possibility of many answers. With a question as simple as this, every student probably has at least one suggestion. The vocabulary for this kind of a lesson can go anywhere, but will probably focus on everyday items.

SOURCE	It was a very hot day and everyone was having trouble concentrating.
TYPE	Expressing opinions
GRAMMAR FOCUS	Present tense, third person and future tense
TO BEGIN	Tell students you have a problem. Wipe your brow, tug at your clothes, and complain to the students that you are hot. Point to the direction of the sun. Ask students, "What do you do when it's hot?" If no one has a answer, draw the first symbol on the chalkboard and pantomime putting on a hat.
CHALK TALK	1. **The teacher wears a hat.**
	2. **_____ stands in the shade.**
	3. **_____ drinks iced tea or has a beer.**
	4. **_____ takes off his/her clothes.**
	5. **_____ uses a fan.**
	6. **_____ goes swimming.**
TO FOLLOW UP	Conduct a Total Physical Response (TPR) lesson. Call out the commands both in the order written and in a different order and have them pantomime the actions.
	Ask students to change these sentences to the future using "After class..." For example, "After class I'm going to put on a hat."
	Have students draw what they do on a cold day or a rainy day and share their answers in pairs.

What Do You Do On a Hot Day?

What Are You Afraid Of?

Jo-Ann Andress, a teacher in a Chalk Talks workshop, shared this lesson that she had done with her elementary school class. It was interesting to me that the list did not change much when I did the same lesson with my adult students. This lesson generated a lot of laughter as students became more and more honest about both small and large fears. With lessons where a symbol can represent the question which has many answers or responses, I sometimes draw the symbol representing a question in the center of the chalkboard with the symbols representing the responses of the students symbols around it.

SOURCE
A small spider had started a chain reaction of screams across a third-grade class.

TYPE
Expressing opinions

GRAMMAR FOCUS
Nouns

TO BEGIN
Play-act being afraid of a spider or bring in an assortment of pictures of spiders or plastic ones. Draw the center symbol on the chalkboard and ask, "What are you afraid of?"

CHALK TALK
1. **Earthquakes.**

2. **Airplane crashes.**

3. **Fires.**

4. **Spiders and bugs.**

5. **Snakes.**

6. **Gangs.**

7. **Having a nightmare.**

8. **Being lost.**

TO FOLLOW UP
For a short follow-up have students draw their own "top five" list of fears and share them with a partner. For several longer follow-up lessons, take each fear and have students brainstorm what logical actions one can take to combat the fear.

What Are You Afraid Of?

   Permission granted to reproduce for classroom use only.

Where Do You Speak English?

This lesson can be done two ways. The first is as a general assessment to learn where students already use English. It also gives students an opportunity to show how they have already been successful using English. A second lesson with similar symbols, "Where Do You Need to Speak English?" can serve as a needs assessment for the teacher planning lessons around the individual needs of the class. If students do not mention using English on the bus, for example, that kind of lesson may best be taught after more urgent needs are met.

SOURCE This was a short brainstorming session on the different places one can speak English.

TYPE Expressing opinions

GRAMMAR FOCUS Prepositional phrases

TO BEGIN First ask students, "How many of you speak a little English?" Next, ask, "Where do you speak English?" If no one volunteers, draw symbol 1 and ask, "Do you speak English at work?"

CHALK TALK 1. At work.

2. On the telephone.

3. At a hospital, at the doctor's.

4. At school.

5. At stores.

6. At parties.

TO FOLLOW UP Take one of the above topics, such as use of the telephone, and brainstorm a list of more specific ideas of uses of English. For example, more specific ideas for using English on the telephone, student responses might be "making a long distance phone call, ordering fast food, asking about a bill," etc.

Where Do You Speak English?

 Permission granted to reproduce for classroom use only.

What If You Won the Lottery?

This is a lesson to use at the end of class when there's about ten minutes left. One day I asked my students if any of them had bought a lottery ticket. A student produced one out of his wallet. First we talked about winning and losing. A big smile was the symbol for winning and a dollar bill with wings on it was the symbol for losing. I then asked them what they would do if they won. While the person who gave the suggestion said, "I would...," we practiced the sentences in third person using names of the class members who gave the suggestions.

SOURCE This exercise was taken from a list of ideas for lessons on expressing opinions. Many of these are short enough that they can be done in ten minutes or less. (See page 12 for other lessons of this type.)

TYPE Expressing opinions

GRAMMAR FOCUS Conditional

TO BEGIN Show students a lottery ticket or talk about different ways to gamble. Draw a symbol for winning and losing money.

CHALK TALK

1. _____ would buy a house.

2. _____ would take a trip.

3. _____ would send money to his/her country.

4. _____ would buy a business.

5. _____ would give money to charity.

6. _____ would buy a present for everyone he/she knows.

TO FOLLOW UP Brainstorm a more specific list for each one of the items. What kind of a house would _____ buy? Where would _____ go on his/her trip? What would _____ buy for everyone?

What If You Won the Lottery?

Permission granted to reproduce for classroom use only.

Getting Ready for the Chinese New Year

Jean Au, an elementary school teacher who was in my drawing workshop, conducted this lesson in her third grade class. A lesson such as this allows every ethnic group to have its moment. All that the teacher has to do is encourage students to tell about themselves, a special event or a holiday in their homeland.

SOURCE	The Chinese New Year was approaching. Two Chinese students from Vietnam shared their New Year's customs.
TYPE	Relating a story
GRAMMAR FOCUS	Present tense, third person plural
TO BEGIN	Hold up a calendar. Talk about different holidays and how people get ready for them.
CHALK TALK	1. We clean the house.
	2. We put up red scrolls for good luck.
	3. We put away sharp objects.
	4. We buy new clothes.
	5. We pay our debts.
	6. We buy special food.
TO FOLLOW UP	Ask the class what the reasons might be for each of these customs. Discuss other New Year's traditions in other cultures. Have students draw symbols to depict their own particular New Year's customs.

Getting Ready for the Chinese New Year

1.
2.
3.
4.
5.
6.

Permission granted to reproduce for classroom use only.

Pak-il, the 100th-Day Birthday

Elaine Sunoo, an ESL teacher who does many cross-cultural activities with her students, shared this lesson in a Chalk Talks workshop. Many cultures have ways of marking the time when newborn babies have survived their first few months. Like many traditions, this Korean one is still practiced although the historical reason has mostly passed.

SOURCE   This lesson grew out of a discussion of different kinds of birthday celebrations. The teacher shared one tradition she was familiar with.

TYPE   Relating a story

GRAMMAR FOCUS   Present tense, third person plural

TO BEGIN   Draw a picture of a birthday cake and candles. Talk about birthdays, when people celebrate them and what they do.

CHALK TALK   1. **In Korea, a long time ago, when times were difficult, many babies did not survive.**

2. **When a baby reached his or her 100th day, it was a special event.**

3. **The family had a big celebration.**

4. **They ate fruit and rice cakes.**

5. **They put their baby next to a paintbrush, a pen, and some money.**

6. **If the baby touched the brush, he would be an artist.**

7. **If the baby touched the pen, he would be a writer.**

8. **If the baby touched the money, he would be a businessman.**

TO FOLLOW UP   Ask the class what the reasons might be for each of these customs. Discuss other birthday or baby traditions in other cultures. Have students draw symbols to depict their own particular birthday customs.

Pak-il, the 100th-Day Birthday

Vietnamese Childbirth Customs

Holly Cress, a teacher who took a Chalk Talks workshop, did this lesson with her students and shared it with me. It was very exciting to see the variety of lessons that probably would not take place without the ability to put symbols on the board. If you do this lesson or one similar to it, expect a lively discussion on childbirth customs and their origins.

SOURCE There was a pregnant woman in a class of mostly women.

TYPE Relating a story

GRAMMAR FOCUS Modals

TO BEGIN Talk about different childbirth customs in the United States. Ask, "What are some childbirth customs in your country?" To focus students' attention, draw a picture of a pregnant woman on the chalkboard.

CHALK TALK **1. A pregnant woman may go to a fortune teller.**

2. After the baby is born, the mother cannot go out.

3. She cannot bathe or shower or brush her teeth.

4. She must do this for one month.

5. Then everyone has a party.

TO FOLLOW UP Have students draw two or three childbirth customs from their homelands. Have student volunteers share their drawings with the class and tell them about these customs.

Vietnamese Childbirth Customs

1.

2.

3.

4.

5.

_____

_____

_____

_____

_____

_____

_____

   Permission granted to reproduce for classroom use only.

The Story of Martin Luther King, Jr.

Many of my students knew something about this great civil rights leader. After drawing the story and using symbols to teach words such as boycott, integration, *and* non-violent protest, *students talked about injustices they see today.*

SOURCE	Martin Luther King's birthday was the following week, and students were going to have the day off.
TYPE	Relating a story
GRAMMAR FOCUS	Past tense, passive voice
TO BEGIN	Draw Symbol 1 on the board or bring in a picture of Martin Luther King, Jr. Ask students to tell you what they know about him.
CHALK TALK	1. **Martin Luther King, Jr. was a third generation African-American minister.**
	2. **He believed in non-violent change.**
	3. **In 1956 black people had to sit at the back of the buses in Montgomery, Alabama.**
	4. **King organized a boycott of the buses.**
	5. **No black people rode the buses for over one year.**
	6. **Finally, the buses were integrated.**
	7. **King also worked for the voting rights of black people.**
	8. **At age 39, he was murdered by James Earl Ray.**
TO FOLLOW UP	Have student volunteers put on a short play of King's life. Assign students different roles. As one student reads the story, the others act it out in pantomime. Include other facts about him, such as where he lived, who he married, etc.

The Story of Martin Luther King, Jr.

Permission granted to reproduce for classroom use only.

How to Stay Healthy

This lesson grew naturally out of a health unit about going to the doctor. Both teacher and students added their opinions. I was the one who added the seatbelt dictum at the end. Be prepared for answers such as, "Get a good husband." Or, "Have less than four children." There was also much heated debate about what constituted good food. As each sentence is practiced, the teacher can attribute the idea to the person who said it.

SOURCE	The class had been learning about going to the doctor.
TYPE	Expressing opinions
GRAMMAR FOCUS	Imperative mode

TO BEGIN   Talk about how to avoid getting sick. Ask, "What are some ways we can stay healthy." To focus students' attention, draw a symbol of a doctor and draw an "X" through it.

CHALK TALK

1. **Eat lots of fruits and vegetables.**

2. **Eat less oil and fat.**

3. **Get plenty of exercise.**

4. **See the doctor once a year.**

5. **Take a break from work.**

6. **Fasten your seat belt.**

TO FOLLOW UP   Have students bring in pictures of healthy and not-so-healthy foods. Glue the pictures onto two sheets of butcher paper. Label the pictures.

1.

2.

3.

4.

5.

6.

Permission granted to reproduce for classroom use only.

How Chin Sprained Her Ankle

This is one of many possible spontaneous lessons that can occur when a student comes to class with something obviously different about herself. Teachers need to be aware, however, that in many cultures it is inappropriate or rude to call attention to physical problems or disabilities. Before one does this type of lesson, it is best to ask the student privately for permission to be the focus. I have never had a student refuse. It is my feeling they are very pleased to learn the English needed to tell their story.

SOURCE	A student comes into the classroom with an bandaged ankle.
TYPE	Relating a story
GRAMMAR FOCUS	Simple past tense

TO BEGIN Express concern to the student who comes in with a new physical problem. Ask, "How did this happen?"

CHALK TALK
1. Chin had a lot of laundry to do yesterday.

2. Her washing machine is in the basement.

3. She carried the laundry down the stairs...

4. ...and fell!

5. The doctor wrapped a bandage around her ankle.

6. Now her husband does the laundry.

TO FOLLOW UP Brainstorm a list of household chores. Have each student write down the list in symbols or words on a piece of paper. Divide students into pairs and have them interview each other asking, "Who does this chore in your house?" Have students write the kinship term (mother, father, husband, wife, etc.) under the symbol or word. As a whole class, have students share their answers.

How Chin Sprained Her Ankle

A Fire in the Apartment

This lesson was done by a teacher in a Chalk Talks workshop. Although this really did happen to a student, it can also be done as a fire safety lesson.

SOURCE	A student came to class one Monday morning and told of a fire in her apartment.
TYPE	Relating a story
GRAMMAR FOCUS	Past tense
TO BEGIN	Draw the symbol for fire. (See page 114.) Ask students, "Has anyone ever had a fire in their apartment?"
CHALK TALK	1. Marta was sleeping in her bedroom. 1. There was a fire in her kitchen. 3. She woke up because she smelled smoke. 4. She saw smoking coming through the door. 5. She crawled over to the door. 6. She felt the door...it was hot. 7. She crawled away from the door... 8. ...and screamed out of the window.
TO FOLLOW UP	Talk about what to do in case of a fire at home, at school or in a car. Arrange for a firefighter to come to your class to talk about fire safety.

A Fire in the Apartment

Using Water Wisely

Etta Collons, a teacher in a Chalk Talks workshop shared this lesson. While it was done with a high school class, like most Chalk Talks lessons, it is adaptable to any grade level. Also, be prepared for students to come up with many ideas.

SOURCE The city had begun a recycling program which led to a discussion about saving water as well.

TYPE Expressing opinions

GRAMMAR FOCUS Imperative mode

TO BEGIN Focus students' attention by bringing in a glass of water or drawing it on the chalkboard and asking, "What are some ways we can save water?"

CHALK TALK
1. **Use special devices in the toilet.**

2. **Do not throw waste paper in the toilet.**

3. **Shower for five minutes or less.**

4. **If you have a only a few dirty dishes, wash them in the sink.**

5. **Fix all leaks.**

6. **When you brush your teeth, turn off the water.**

TO FOLLOW UP Make a chart with good ideas for saving water and other natural resources. Have students draw pictures or cut them out of a magazine to place on the chart.

Invite someone from the Department of Water and Power to come speak to the class about water and energy conservation. After the talk, add more ideas to your chart.

Using Water Wisely

_____

_____

_____

_____

_____

_____

_____

CHALK TALKS

Permission granted to reproduce for classroom use only.

Looking for Work

One day, a student, Odilia Mendez, asked me if I knew of any jobs in the area. This list was gleaned from the brainstorming session that followed. Teachers need to encourage student suggestions, especially since adult students are often a great resource of job possibilities. The question "What can _____ do?" posed to the class in response to a real student problem, can lead to wonderful co-operative class-building lessons.

SOURCE	A student came into the classroom with a problem.
TYPE	Expressing opinions
GRAMMAR FOCUS	Can or should
TO BEGIN	Express concern to the student who comes in with a problem. Tell the class the problem and ask, "What can Odilia do?" Draw the first symbol to focus students' attention.
CHALK TALK	**1. Odilia needs a job.**
	2. She can ask her friends about work.
	3. She can look in the newspapers.
	4. She can walk around the city and look in windows for 'Help Wanted' signs.
	5. She can go to an employment agency...
	6. ...or she can start a business from her home.
TO FOLLOW UP	Bring in ads from the newspaper and discuss the meaning of abbreviations in the ads. For a higher level class, involve students in creating a possible dialogue the student can have at the employment agency or with a prospective employer.

Looking for Work

Permission granted to reproduce for classroom use only.

The Job Interview

Many lessons on job interviews focus on the answers a person needs to give about one's life history and work experience. This lesson focuses on questions the prospective employee wants to ask.

SOURCE   We had been doing a unit on job interviews and had concentrated on giving life histories and work experience.

TYPE   Asking for information

GRAMMAR FOCUS   Questions

TO BEGIN   Tell students they were just offered a job in an office or at a factory. Make it as specific as you like. Ask, "What do you want to know about your new job?"

CHALK TALK   1. **What are my responsibilities?**

2. **What hours do I work?**

3. **What is my schedule?**

4. **How much do I make?**

5. **Do I need a car?**

6. **What do I need to wear?**

7. **Is there sick pay or vacation pay?**

8. **Do I get health insurance?**

TO FOLLOW UP   Role-play the job interview. Discuss possible answers to the questions before you begin. Do the role play in front of the class with a student volunteer, using the symbols as cues for the questions. As the boss, take on different personalities. Divide students into pairs and have them switch roles after five or ten minutes.

Permission granted to reproduce for classroom use only.

First Day at Work

This is a natural follow-up lesson to "The Job Interview." Again, it focuses on asking questions. The lesson is general, but depending on the students in the class it can be adapted to be job specific, such as "The First Day Driving a Truck."

SOURCE	After we had done a role play for a job interview, we talked about what we would need to know if we got the job.
TYPE	Asking for information
GRAMMAR FOCUS	Questions

TO BEGIN Tell students this the first day on the job. Ask, "What do you want to know the first day on the new job?"

CHALK TALK

1. Where do I punch in?

2. Where do I put my lunch?

3. Where are the supplies?

4. Who can I ask for information?

5. What time is lunch break?

6. Can you show me how to use this machine?

TO FOLLOW UP Role-play the questions. Discuss possible answers to the questions before you begin. Do the role play in front of the class with a student volunteer, using the symbols as cues for the questions. As the boss or fellow worker, take on different personalities. Divide students into pairs and have them switch roles after five or ten minutes.

First Day at Work

Steps to Paint a House

We had a very lively discussion about the order in which each task is done when you paint a house. This lesson took over an hour because we first practiced saying all the steps. Then we had to come to some kind of consensus as to the proper order. This lesson can take quite a bit of time, and students can suggest even more steps in the sequence than are listed here.

SOURCE	A student had told the class that he works as a painter.
TYPE	Sequencing
GRAMMAR FOCUS	Imperative

TO BEGIN Explain to the class that there are many ways to accomplish the same job. Ask, "What is the first thing a painter does when he paints a house?"

CHALK TALK
1. Choose the color.

2. Buy the paint.

3. Move the furniture.

4. Remove the fixtures.

5. Fix the cracks...

6. ...and wait.

7. Sand the walls.

8. Tape the windows.

9. Paint.

10. Put back the furniture.

11. Put back the fixtures.

12. Take a shower.

TO FOLLOW UP Conduct a TPR (Total Physical Response) lesson. Have students pantomime the sequence to you and then to each other in pairs.

Have students work in groups to sequence another task. Have them choose the task they are going to write about.

Steps to Paint a House

1.
2.
3.
4.
5.
6.
7.
8.
9.
10.
11.
12.

_____

_____

_____

_____

_____

_____

_____

The Dictionary
of Symbols

Basic Facts

In Class

teacher	student	desk
book	chalkboard	computer
chair	pencil	pen

speak

listen

write

read

print

study

People

Vital Statistics

name

address

telephone

age

date of birth

place of birth

sex	height	weight
single	married	divorced
widowed	separated	occupation

Emotions

happy

sad

angry

afraid

embarrassed

confused

hungry/thirsty

surprised

tired

frustrated

nervous

sorry

Occupations and Jobs

apartment
manager

artist

bricklayer

busboy (girl)

businessman
businesswoman

butcher

carpenter

childcare worker

cook/chef

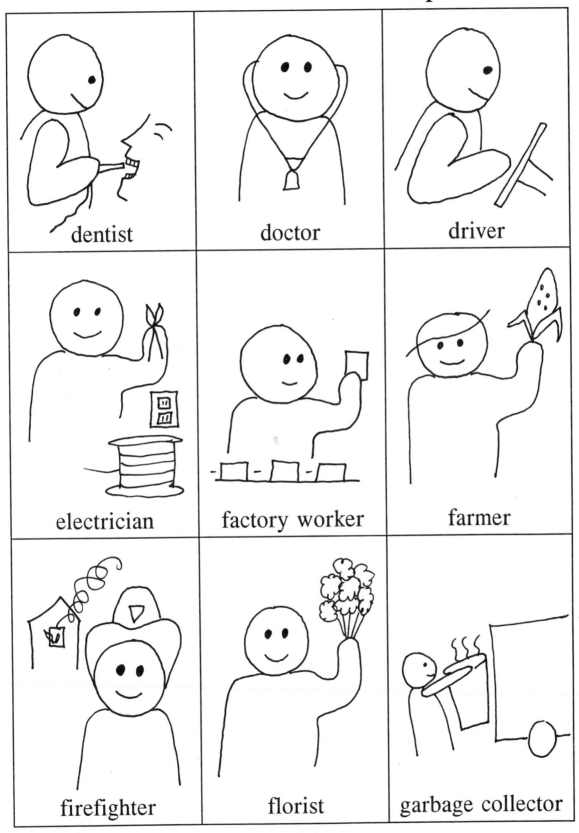

dentist

doctor

driver

electrician

factory worker

farmer

firefighter

florist

garbage collector

Occupations and Jobs

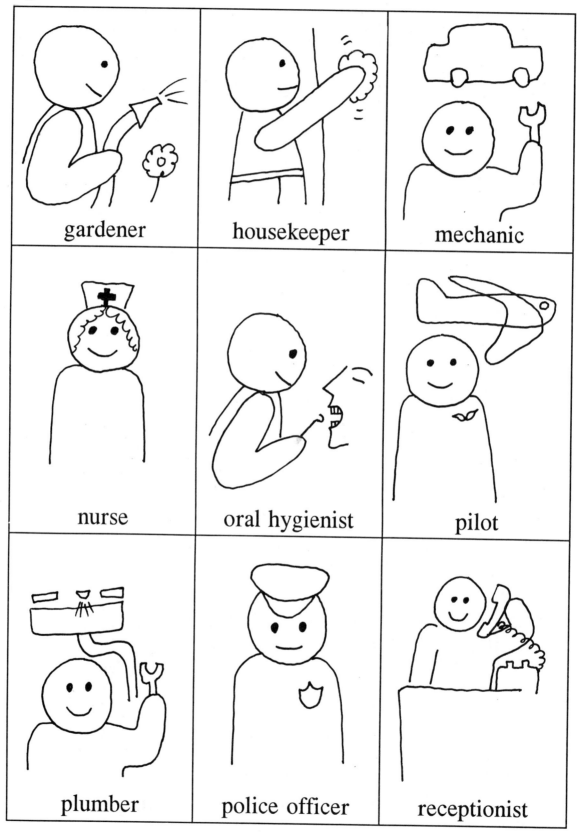

gardener

housekeeper

mechanic

nurse

oral hygienist

pilot

plumber

police officer

receptionist

reporter	seamstress	secretary
singer	soldier	stockboy (girl)
store clerk	teacher	waiter/waitress

Time

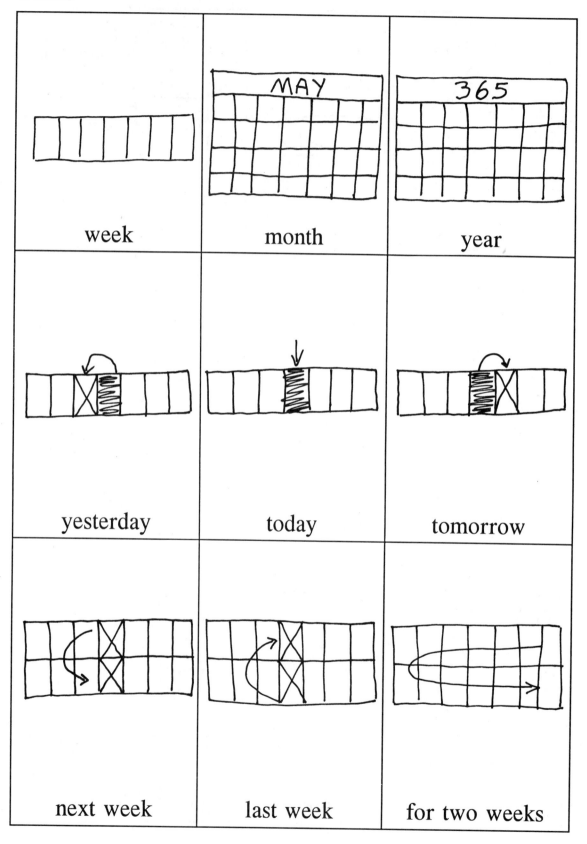

week	month	year
yesterday	today	tomorrow
next week	last week	for two weeks

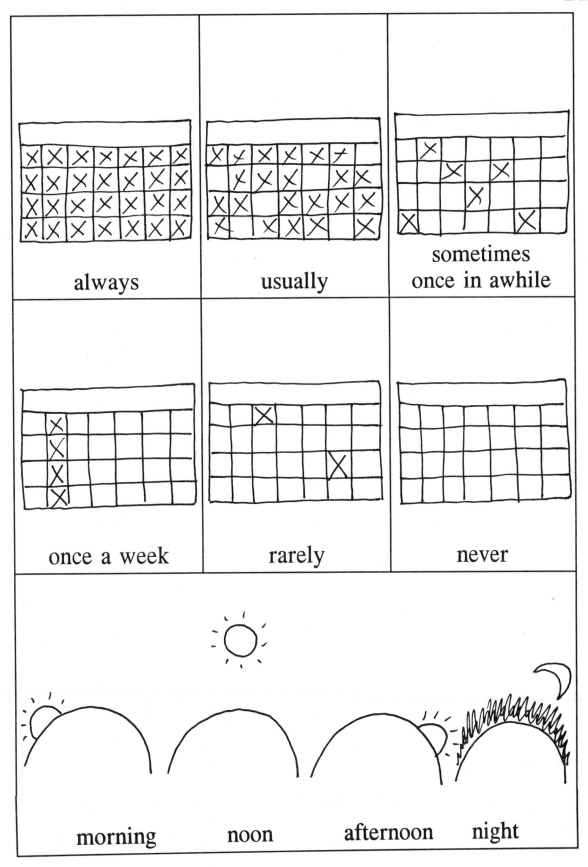

always

usually

sometimes
once in awhile

once a week

rarely

never

morning   noon   afternoon   night

Weather/Seasons

hot

warm

windy

rain

summer

fall

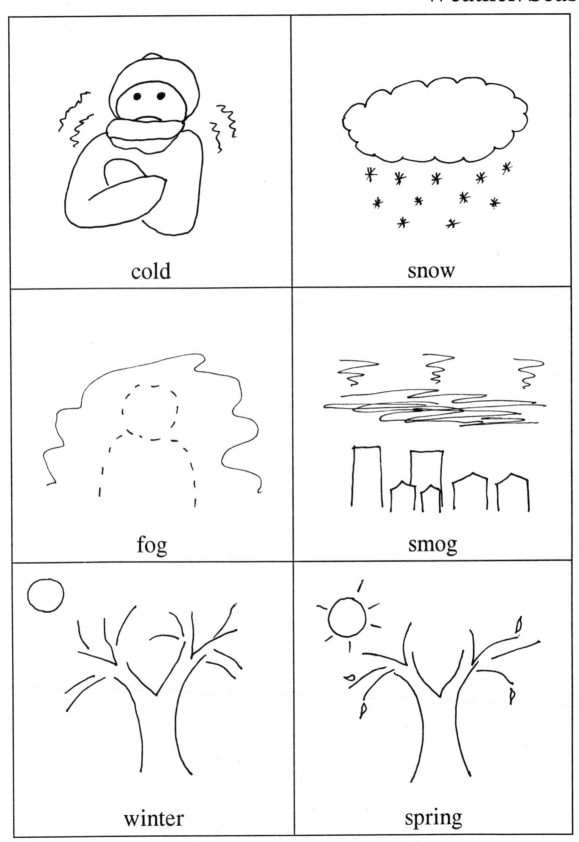

cold

snow

fog

smog

winter

spring

Life Events

birthday

graduation

engagement

wedding

retirement

funeral

have a baby

get a job

join the army

immigrate

move

go to jail

Holidays

New Year's Day

Martin L. King's Birthday

Valentine's Day

Presidents' Day

Easter

July 4th

Halloween

Thanksgiving

Christmas

Natural Disasters

earthquake

fire

flood

hurricane

tornado

volcanic eruption

Verbs

116 - 126

Verbs

breathe

grow

eat

drink

see

hear

116

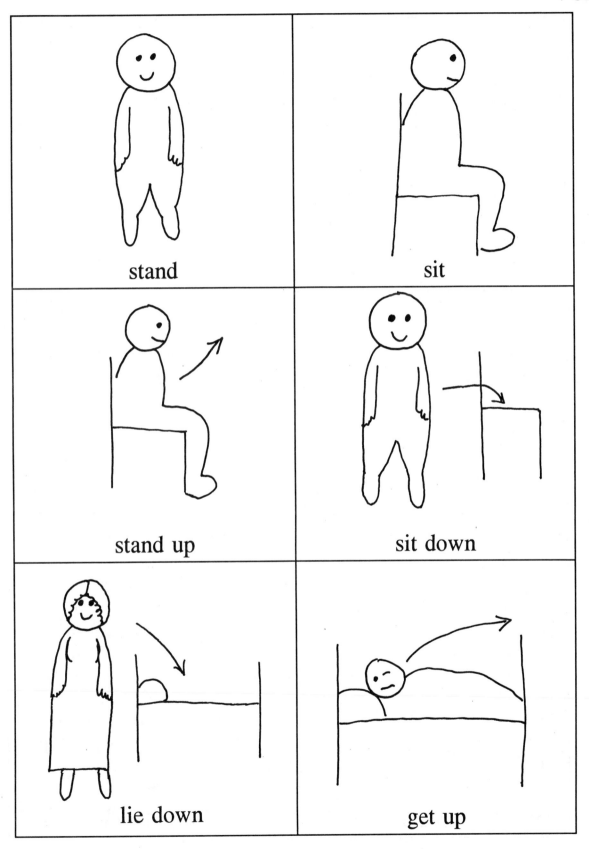

stand

sit

stand up

sit down

lie down

get up

Verbs

get dressed

get undressed

sleep

make love

dream

have a nightmare

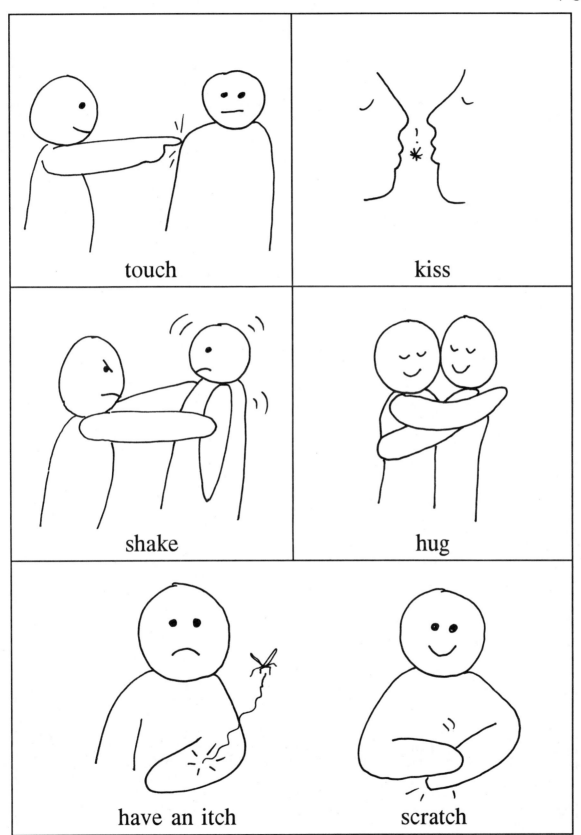

touch

kiss

shake

hug

have an itch

scratch

Verbs

sing

play the piano

watch TV

see a movie

paint

draw

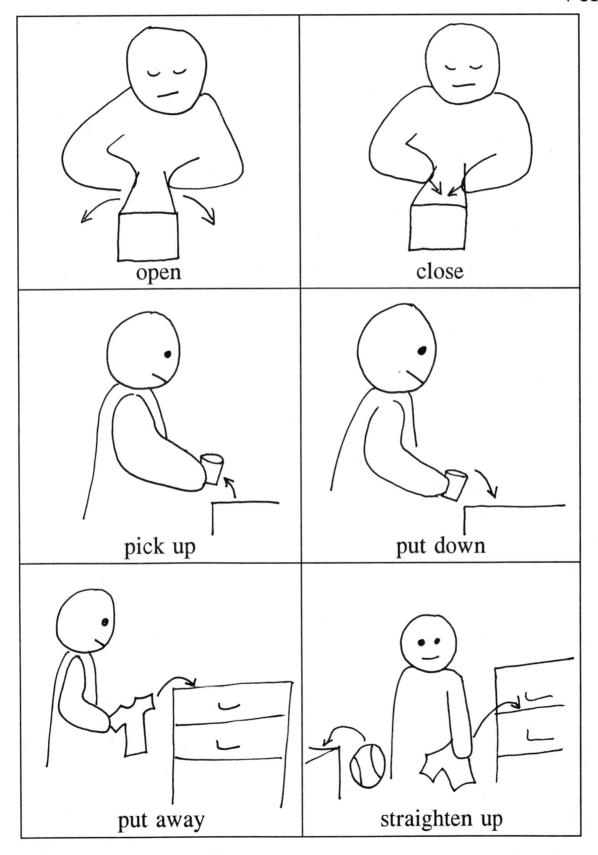

open

close

pick up

put down

put away

straighten up

Verbs

stay at home

go

drive

take the bus

arrive/come

leave

walk

run

fly

jump

dance

crawl

Verbs

ride a bicycle

play

swim

ski

climb

fall

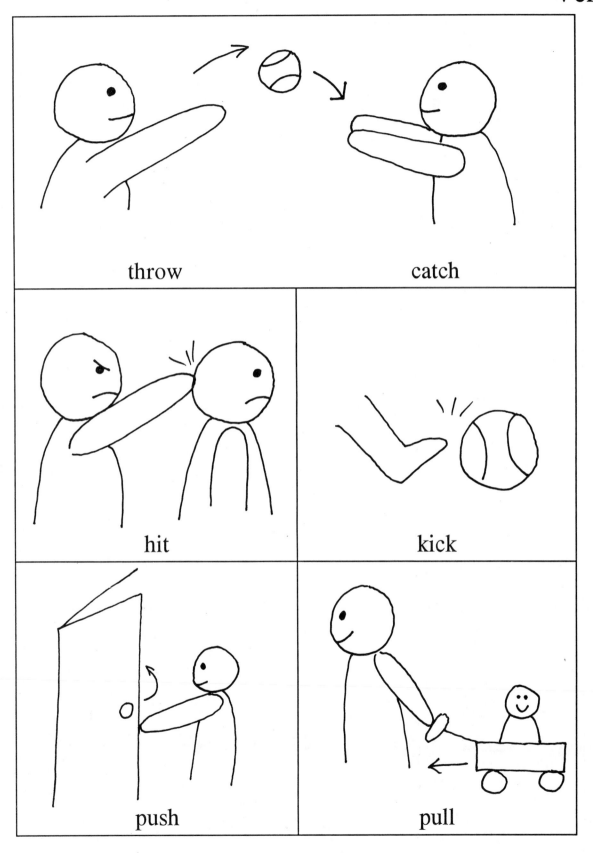

throw

catch

hit

kick

push

pull

Verbs

give

receive/get

carry

build

break

fix

Health

The Body

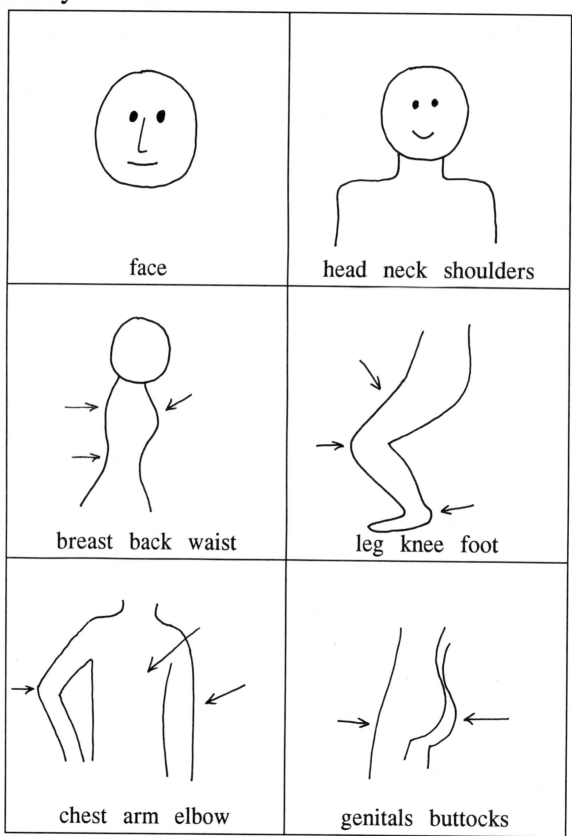

face

head neck shoulders

breast back waist

leg knee foot

chest arm elbow

genitals buttocks

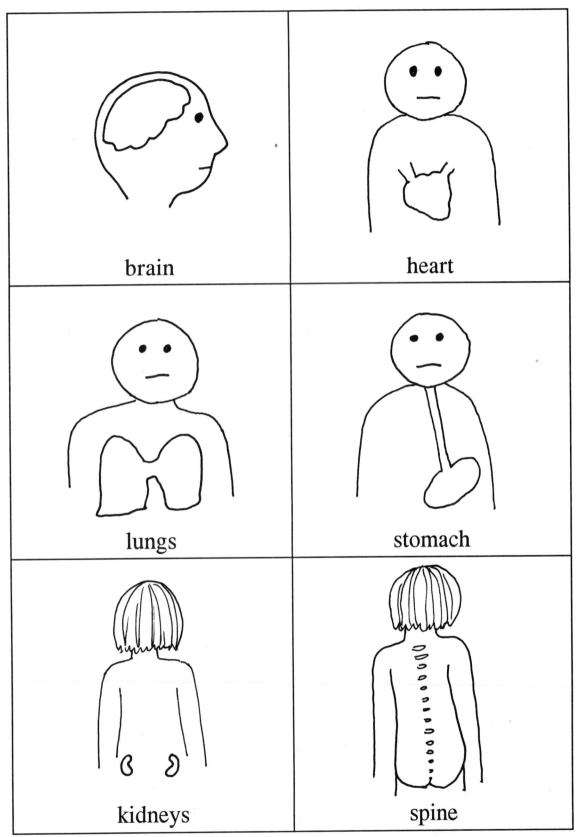

brain

heart

lungs

stomach

kidneys

spine

Personal Hygiene

have body odor

take a shower

wash hair

shave

use the toilet

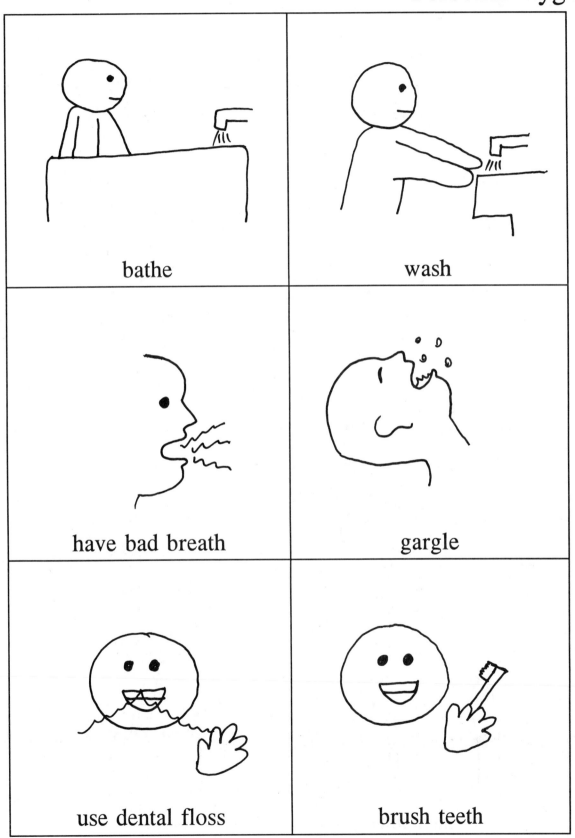

bathe

wash

have bad breath

gargle

use dental floss

brush teeth

Aches and Pains

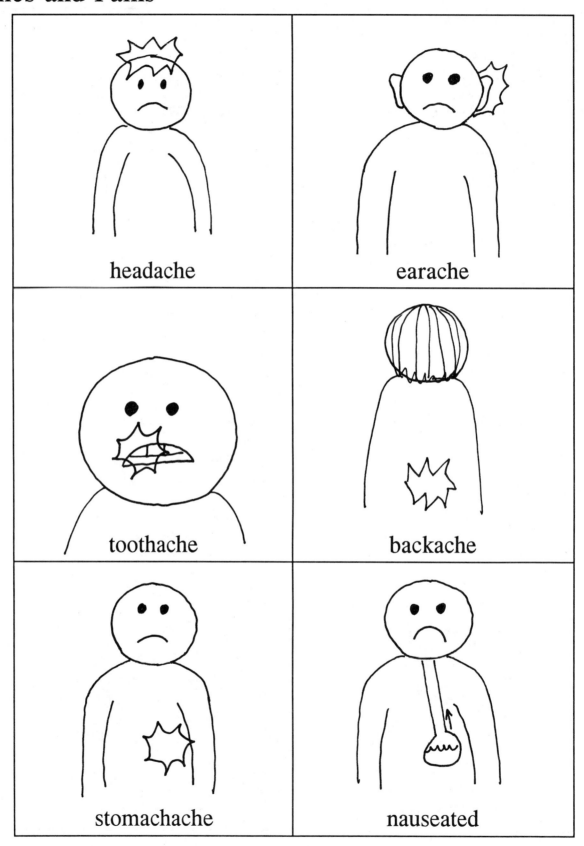

headache

earache

toothache

backache

stomachache

nauseated

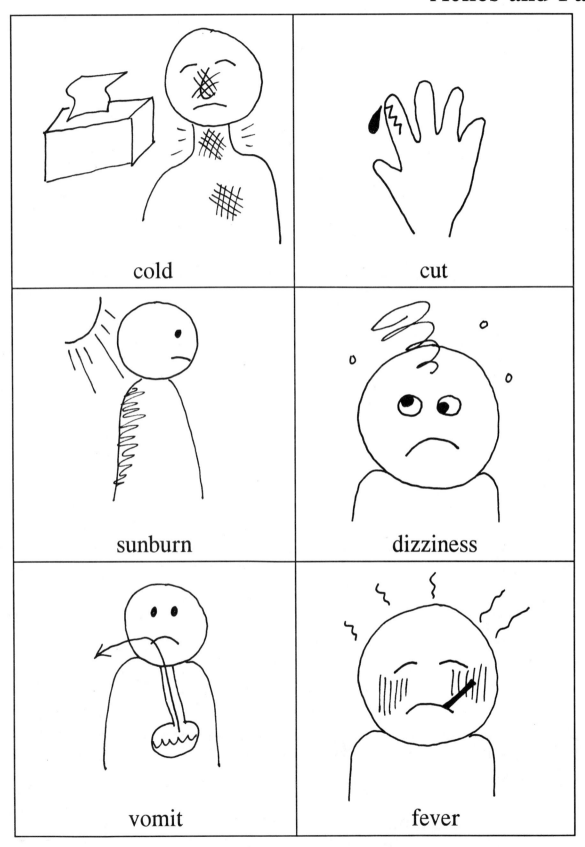

cold

cut

sunburn

dizziness

vomit

fever

At the Doctor's

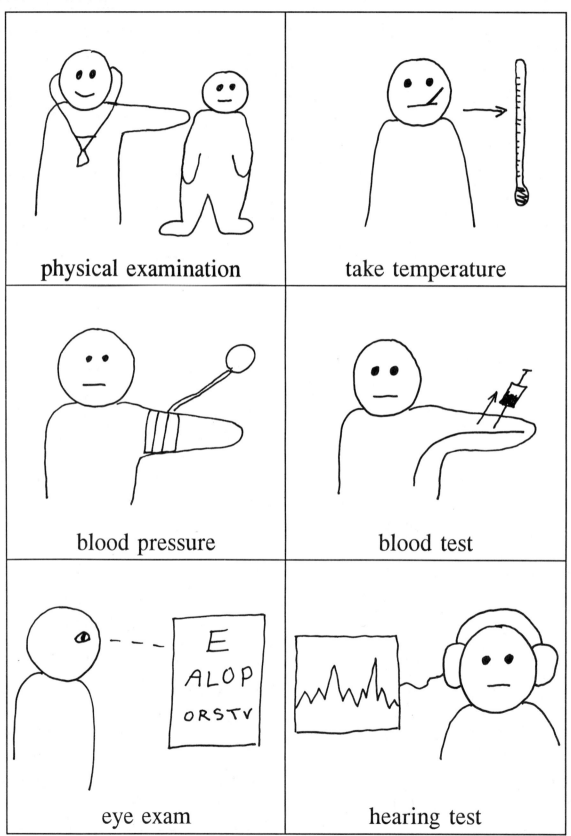

physical examination

take temperature

blood pressure

blood test

eye exam

hearing test

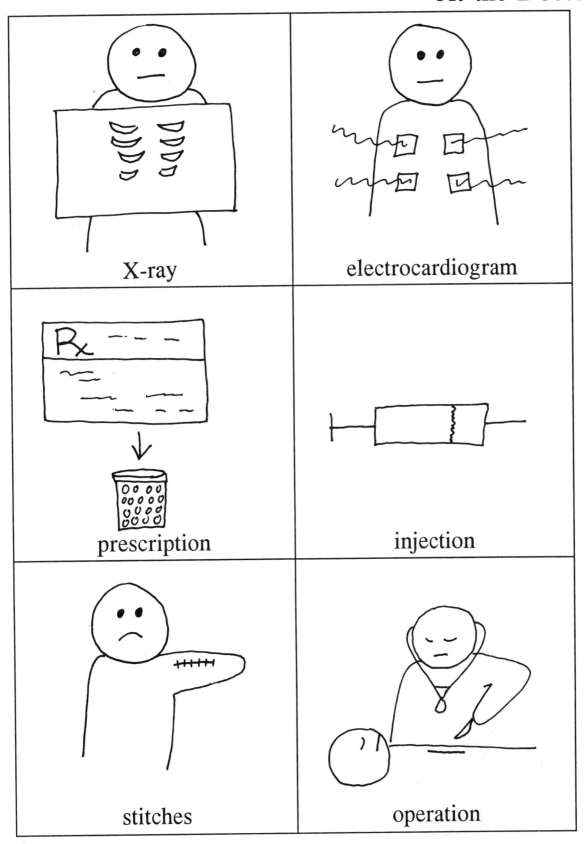

X-ray

electrocardiogram

prescription

injection

stitches

operation

Pregnancy and Childbirth

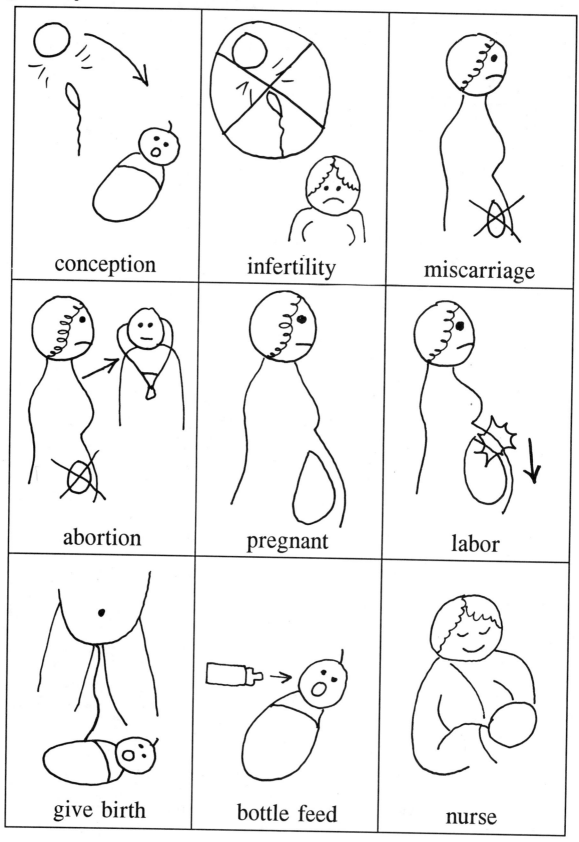

conception	infertility	miscarriage
abortion	pregnant	labor
give birth	bottle feed	nurse

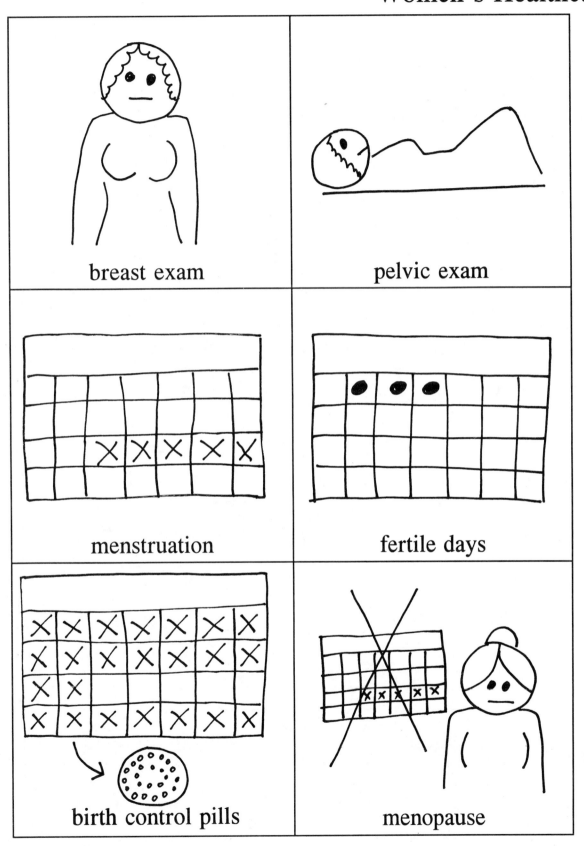

breast exam

pelvic exam

menstruation

fertile days

birth control pills

menopause

Emergencies

be burned

be choking

be bleeding

be wounded

be drowning

138

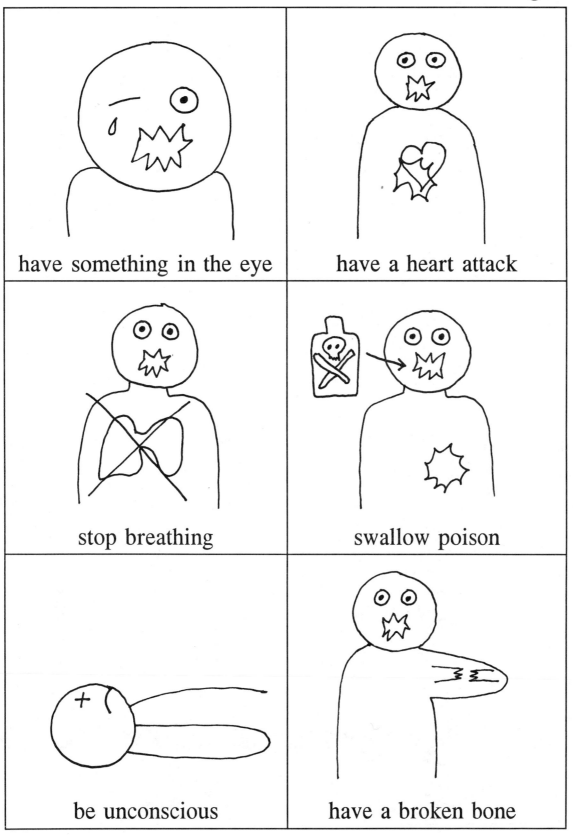

have something in the eye

have a heart attack

stop breathing

swallow poison

be unconscious

have a broken bone

Health Aids

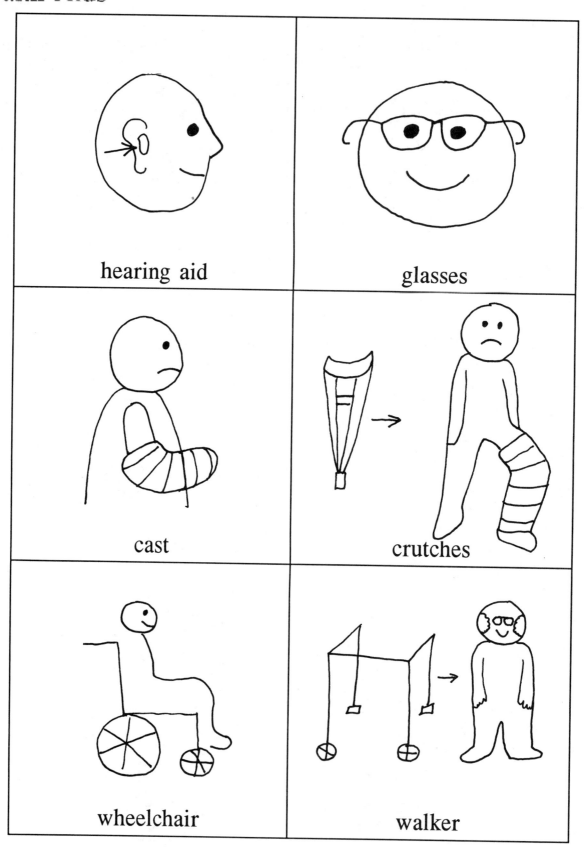

hearing aid

glasses

cast

crutches

wheelchair

walker

At Home

Places to Live

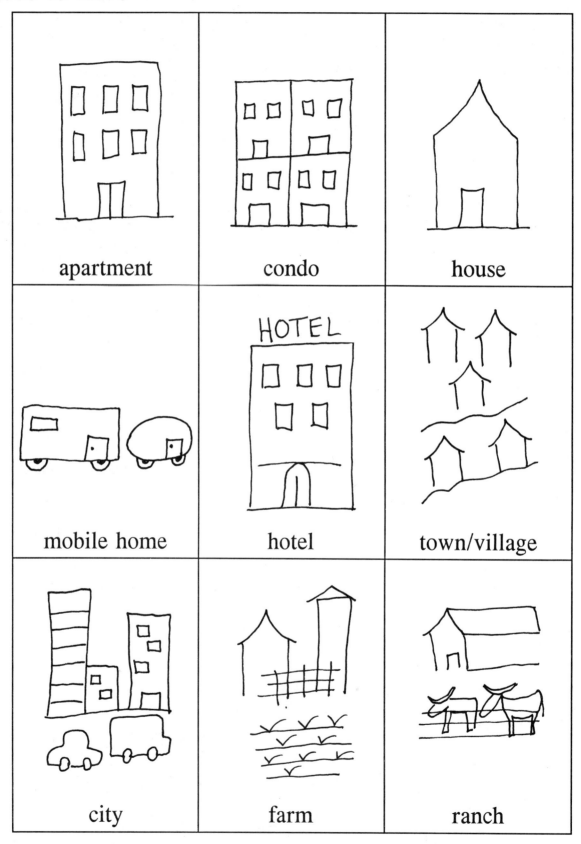

apartment	condo	house
mobile home	hotel	town/village
city	farm	ranch

attic

living room

dining room

kitchen

family room

bedroom

bathroom

garage

basement

In the Kitchen

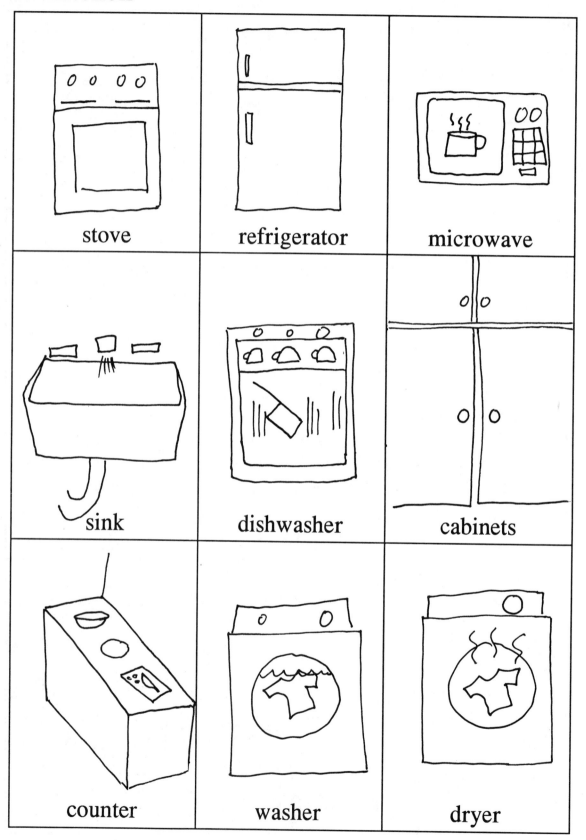

stove

refrigerator

microwave

sink

dishwasher

cabinets

counter

washer

dryer

air conditioner

heater (radiator)

furnace

bed

bathtub

dresser

piano

sofa

table

In the House

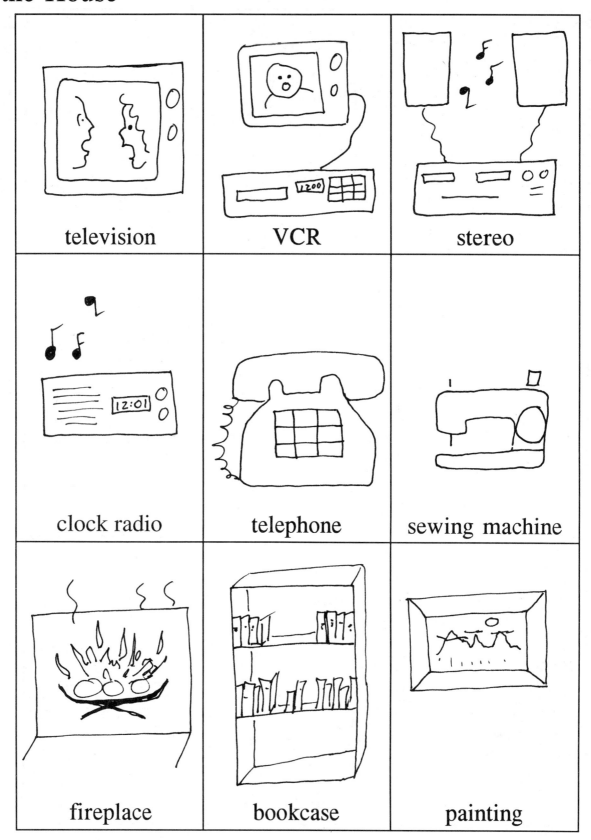

television

VCR

stereo

clock radio

telephone

sewing machine

fireplace

bookcase

painting

camera

photograph

statue

fan

lamp

curtains

scissors

keys

lightbulb

Household Chores

wash dishes

clean

do laundry

make beds

sweep

wash floors

Tools

clamp	drill	flashlight
hammer	nail	paintbrush
pliers	saw	screw
screwdriver	tape measure	wrench

Garden/Outside

cut	dig	harvest
pick	plant	water
hose	sprinklers	shovel
wheelbarrow	lawnmower	rake

wheat

corn

rice

flowers

bushes

trees

Childcare

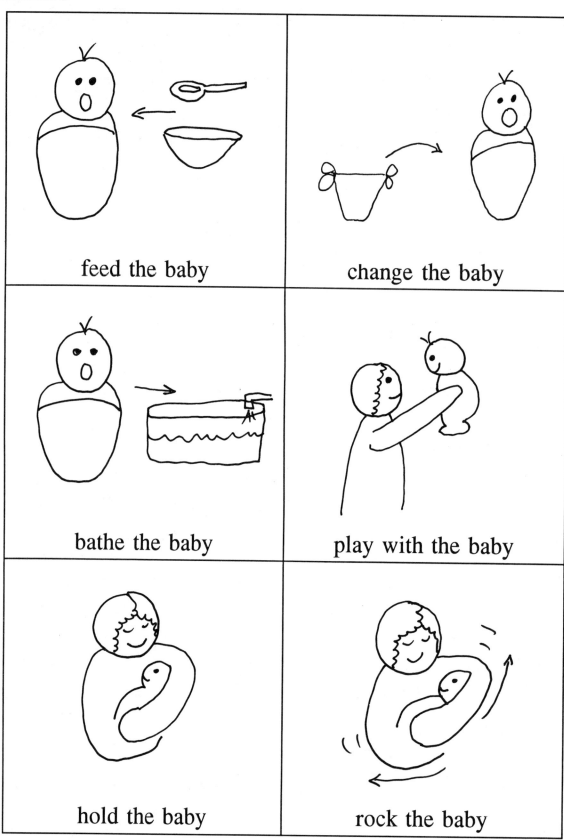

feed the baby

change the baby

bathe the baby

play with the baby

hold the baby

rock the baby

Food and Clothing

Cooking Verbs

bake	barbecue	boil
broil	fry	microwave
mix	sauté	steam

Food

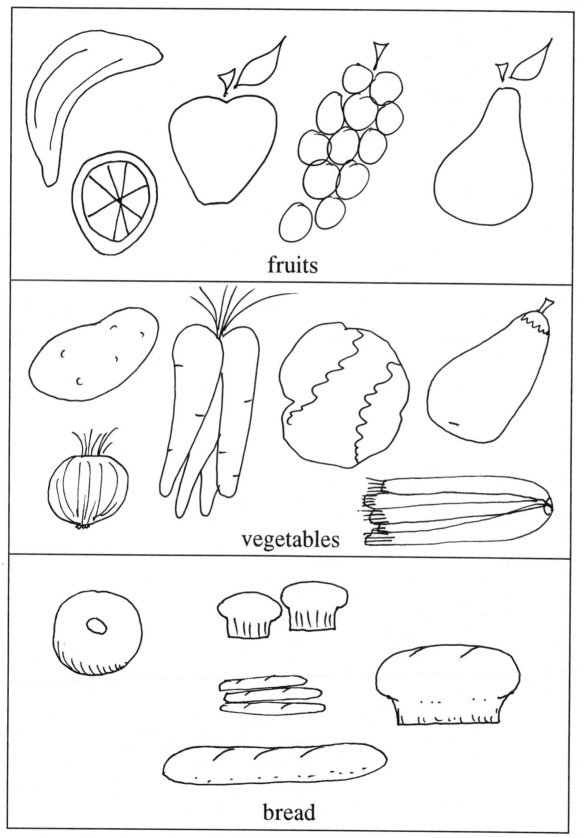

fruits

vegetables

bread

Food

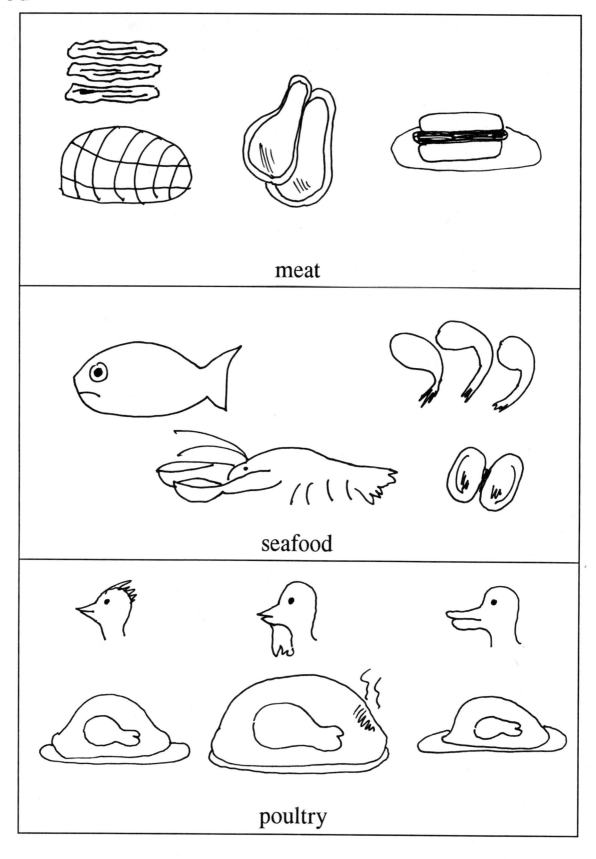

meat

seafood

poultry

Food

dairy

drinks

sweets

Prepared Foods

burrito

French fries

hamburger

hot dog

pizza

spaghetti

basket	bottle	bowl
can	carton	cup
glass	jar	pail/bucket

Clothing

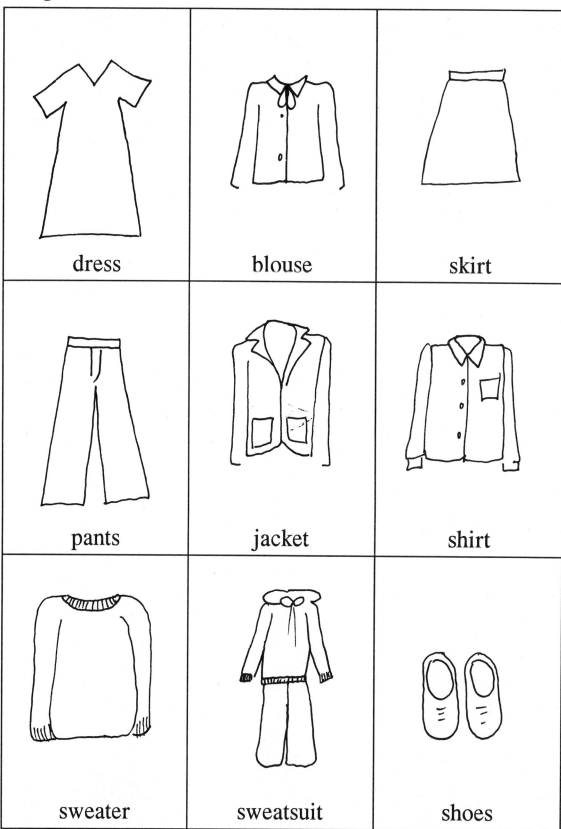

dress	blouse	skirt
pants	jacket	shirt
sweater	sweatsuit	shoes

160

hat

scarf

gloves

belt

wallet

purse

socks   pantyhose

underwear

bra   slip

Clothing

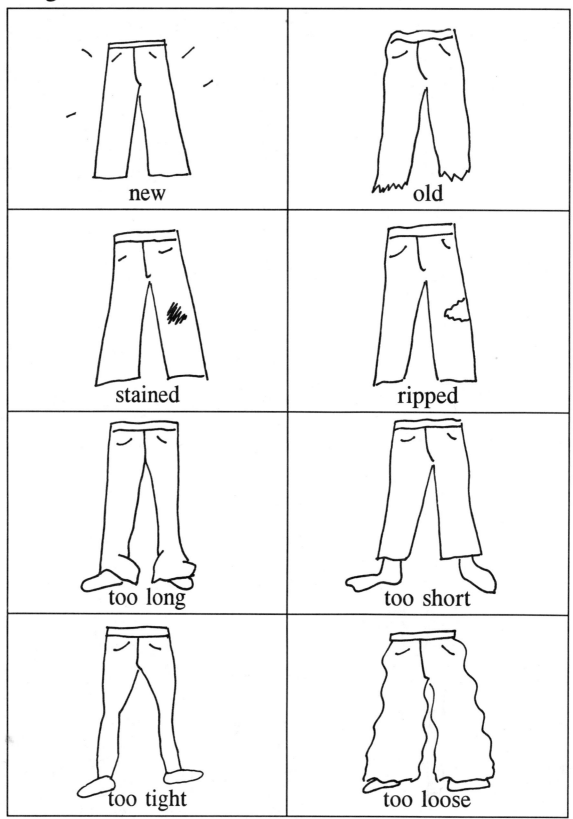

new

old

stained

ripped

too long

too short

too tight

too loose

The Community

Places to Go

baseball game

beach

countryside

dance

mountains

movies

car races

concert

desert

horse races

park

theater

In the City

bar	bank	drug store
hospital	library	mall
market	police station	post office
restaurant	school	train station

noisy neighbors

traffic

crowded schools

dirty streets

gangs

homeless people

Transportation

airplane	bicycle	boat
bus	car	helicopter
submarine	subway	taxi
tractor	train	truck

out of gas and no oil

dead battery

flat tire

won't start

no brakes

accident

Crime

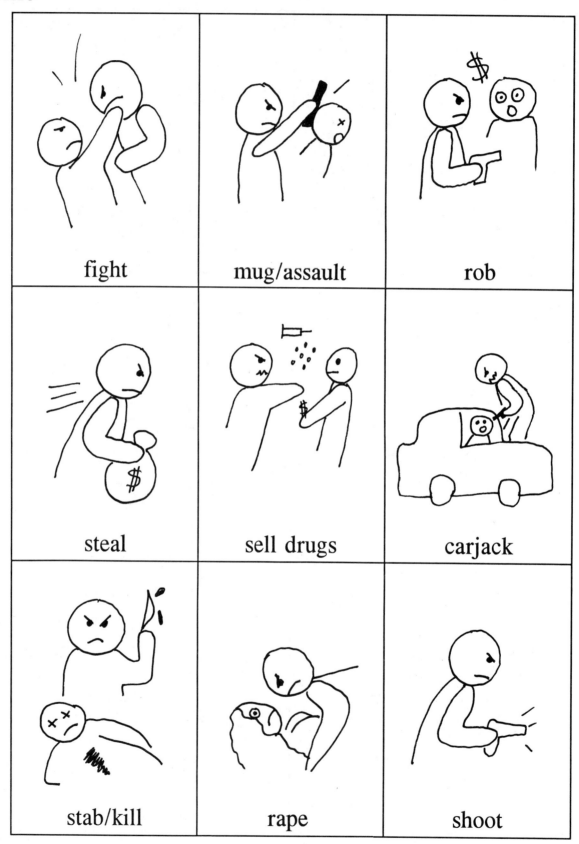

fight

mug/assault

rob

steal

sell drugs

carjack

stab/kill

rape

shoot

1. judge 2. court reporter 3. lawyer
4. witness 5. jury 6. defendant

Animals

bear

lion

tiger

elephant

giraffe

monkey

horse

cow

pig

sheep

donkey

chicken

Animals

dog

cat

bird

rabbit

goat

deer

Grammar

Pronouns

Prepositions

in	on above	next to
up	down	around
in front of	behind	on top of
under	near	far from

Question Words

who?

what?

where?

when?

why?

how?

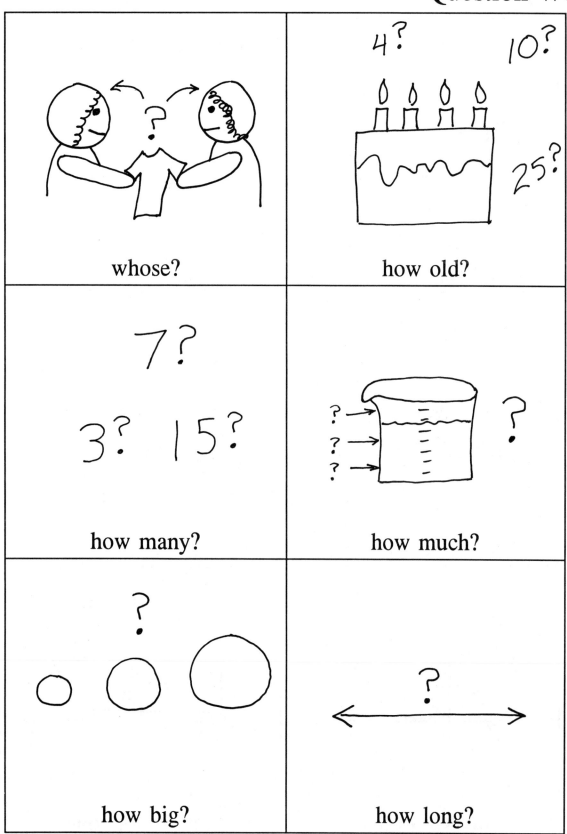

whose?

how old?

how many?

how much?

how big?

how long?

Verb Tenses

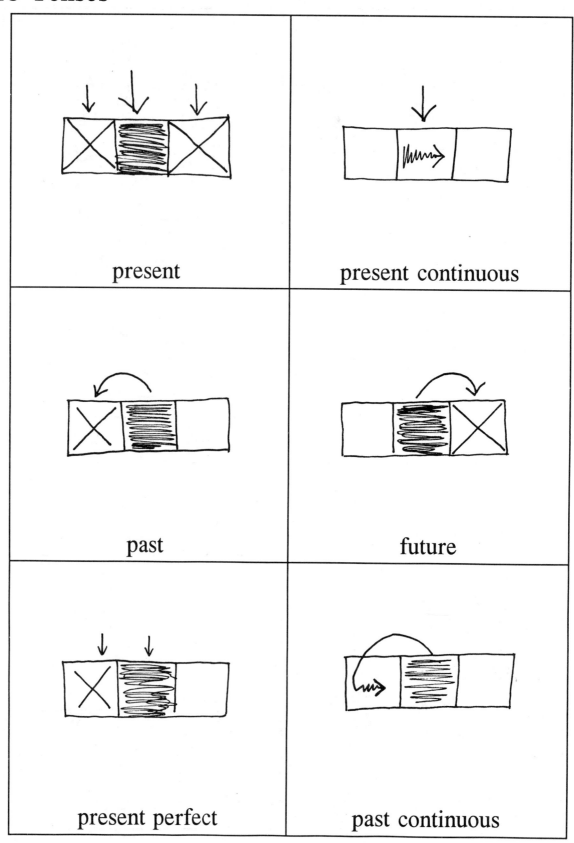

present

present continuous

past

future

present perfect

past continuous

Additional Resources

I am frequently asked in workshops, "Do your students draw too? Isn't there some advantage in having them draw?" The answer is an unqualified yes! Having students draw pictures of their families, their homes, what they like most about school, etc., provides perfect communication starters and can be the beginning of wonderful personal oral and written activities. *Drawing Out* by Sharron Bassano and Mary Ann Christison (San Francisco: Alta Book Center Publishers, 1995) is a photocopiable resource that gives a wealth of lesson ideas which begin with students drawing.

Books I have found helpful as drawing resources are: *Everything You Ever Wanted to Know About Cartooning but Were Afraid to Draw* by Christopher Hart (New York: Watson-Guptill, 1994), which gives easy instructions for making interesting characters, and *1000 Pictures for Teachers to Copy* by Andrew Wright (New York: Addison-Wesley Longman, 1985), an excellent resource for drawing stick figures.

For ESL teachers interested in picture-based textbooks which use drawings in context, see *Going Places: Picture-Based English, Books 1 and 2* by Eric Burton and Lois Maharg (New York: Addison-Wesley Longman, 1995).

Index of Completed Chalk Talks with Teacher's Notes

Índice de símbolos (Spanish Index of Symbols)

English Index of Symbols